# Quilters' Stories
*Collecting History in the Heart of America*

By Deb Rowden

## QUILTERS' STORIES
*Collecting History in the Heart of America*

By Deb Rowden
Edited by Edie McGinnis
Copy edited by Judy Pearlstein
Design by Kelly Ludwig
Portraits by Ray Rowden
Quilt photographs by Krissy Krauser
Illustrations by Gary Embrey Design/Eric Sears
Production assistance by Jo Ann Groves

Published by Kansas City Star Books
1729 Grand Boulevard
Kansas City, Missouri 64108

First edition, first printing
ISBN: 0-9754804-9-9

Printed in the United States of America
By Walsworth Publishing Co.
Marceline, Missouri

To order copies, call StarInfo, 816-234-4636 (say "Operator")

## ★ KANSAS CITY STAR BOOKS

www.PickleDish.com <http://www.pickledish.com/>

The Quilter's Home Page

# Acknowledgements

Thanks to the **quilters** whose stories appear in this book. You shared your valuable time, opened your homes to me and told your stories. Each shared photos and fabric and, on top of it all, a favorite project for others to enjoy. Your enthusiasm, kindness and joy is a rich legacy for us all.

Thanks to **Kansas City Star Books** for supporting this work. The Star has always been a rather magical name for a Midwestern quilter: we continue to find old Star patterns among a beloved relative's sewing possessions (my Aunt Katharine's were in a drawer), and nestled among antiques to this day.

Thanks to **Doug Weaver**. Your calm support makes this work a joy.

Thanks to **Edie McGinnis**. Edie is a great editor, offering just the right blend of encouragement while demanding the best.

Thanks to **Kelly Ludwig**, the design firecracker who makes everything dance across the pages in a most delightful way.

Thanks to **Gary Embrey** and **Eric Sears** for patiently producing excellent illustrations.

Thanks to Star photographer, **Krissy Krauser**, for delivering great shots of these beloved quilts. Thanks also to **Edie McGinnis** and **Sally Morrow** for helping with the photo shoot.

Thanks to **Jo Ann Groves** for art production support. You deliver the best.

Thanks to all **my stitching buddies**. They enrich and enliven my life on a regular basis.

Thanks to my family for their love and support. My husband, **Ray Rowden**, photographed each quilter's portrait—working together with Ray again was quite a pleasure. My dear mom, **Lou Gehlbach**, enthusiastically pitched in to help stitch and test patterns. My dad, **Walt Gehlbach**, surprised us with some of his memories of family quilters. My daughters, **Kate and Betsy**, lent suggestions and advice at helpful moments. Kate even tested one pattern.

Thanks to everyone who suggested a quilter for this book. I would have liked to have talked to everyone mentioned for inclusion.

# Contents

# Introduction

I interviewed 14 quilters for this book.

I truly believe I could have interviewed 14 other quilters and found stories just as diverse and interesting. Then 14 more, and 14 more......

## WHO WAS INTERVIEWED

I think it's important to note that this is not a book of "the best of" quilters. I was given the freedom of talking to people I chose. These are 14 people I was curious about.

Some of these quilters I have been lucky to know for years. They've been my teachers, my fellow stitchers and my friends.

Some I met at our first interview. With a shared interest in quilting, it's amazing how quickly you can become comfortable visiting and trading tales.

I did limit my choices to people who had been quilting for a long time, with a body of work behind them. I was selective based on age more than anything.

Some of these quilters I have admired from afar for many years. It was a bit of a dream come true to visit with them and see a bit of their world.

## WHY I DID THIS

I came to this project out of frustration.

I was editing another book, about women who quilted in days gone by. The author and I were searching and searching for any written information we could find about why those women quilted, about how they felt when they quilted. We kept coming up short.

That's when I dreamed up this book.

I thought of all the people I know right here in the Midwest who have been quilting, teaching us and inspiring fellow quilters for most of our adult lifetimes.

I thought we should start collecting their stories now. Now—while they're here, while they're still actively engaged in their life's creative work.

## MORE STORIES ARE BETTER

I hope readers will consider these stories to be only part of these women's stories. The complete stories of these wonderful quilters would not fit in this book. They could not properly be told by just one person. A grandchild could probably get a different story from their grandmother than anyone else. A quilting friend could supply a totally different side of the story.

I hope people who read these stories will ask the quilters in their lives more questions and write down what they say.

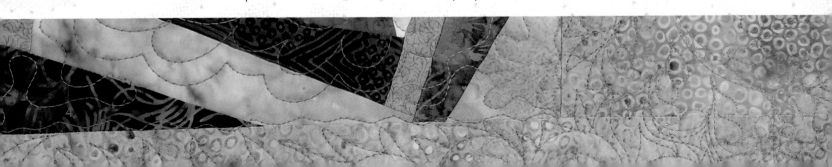

## START ASKING QUESTIONS

Here's the good part.

People enjoy being asked about themselves.

Just by asking questions and being genuinely interested in the answers, you'll be surprised what you hear. Most people find it is fun to get a chance to talk about themselves, to reminisce and ponder how their life has unfolded.

See the section in the back of the book for ways to get started collecting your own quilter's stories.

## TELL YOUR OWN STORY

We are living in a wonderful time for quilting: so many fabrics, classes, magazines and books are available as great sources of inspiration. We find the need to relax with something tactile and colorful as a break from our high-tech, fast-paced lives. The quilters in this book reinforce the notion that this is a treat, something we do for ourselves to replenish our soul.

I don't think this is anything new. Quilting has always been a retreat, a fun place for creative souls to go, to make something beautiful.

Consider capturing some of your own thoughts and history. Keep a log of your quilt projects. Take the time to make notes for your family members: dates, names, etc.

Check the back of the book for more information about how others are collecting this information.

## WHAT YOU'LL FIND IN THE BOOK

You'll find a story about each quilter, based on an interview and additional information they have provided. Each story is followed by a column with factual information.

You'll find a project provided by each quilter. Some are original designs. Some are projects inspired by others. Some celebrate a sentimental quilt passed down by a loved one.

Enjoy!

—*Deb Rowden*
*January, 2005*

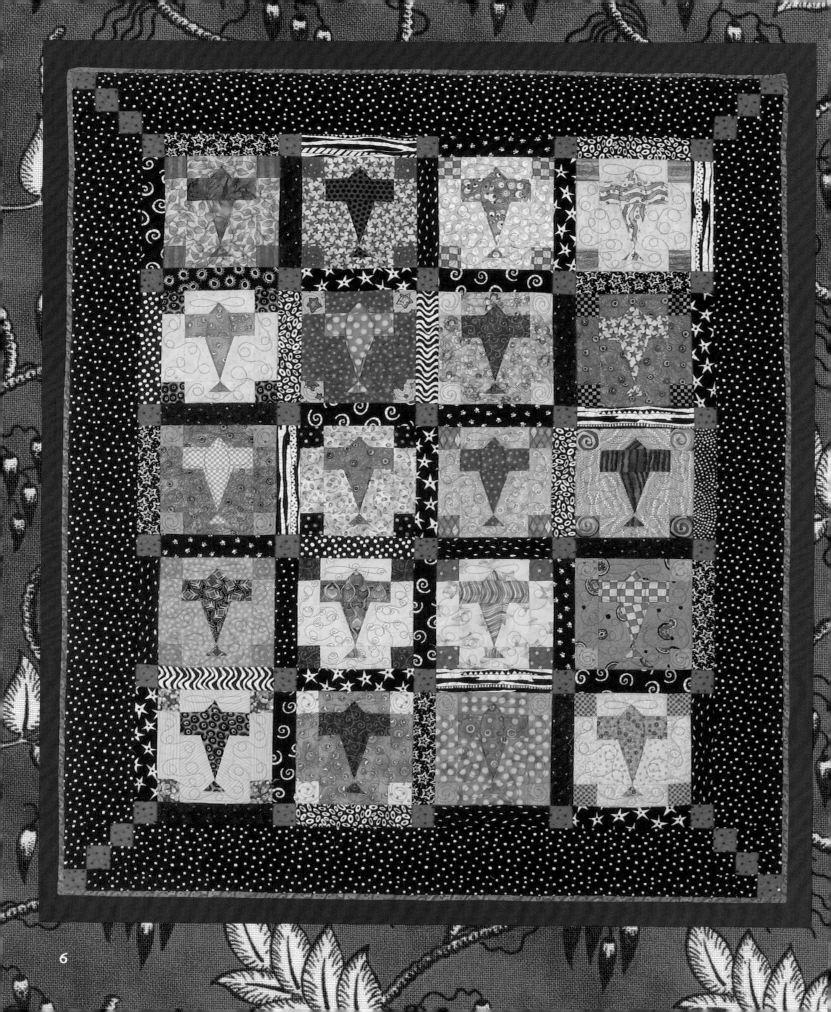

6

*"I'm living in heaven here."*

# Barbara Brackman

**B**arbara Brackman's lifelong dreams included working for a newspaper and designing fabric. She's doing both now.

Her name has run along the selvedge of Moda fabrics since she began designing for them in 1999. She creates several lines of reproduction fabrics every year.

She's written several quilt books for *The Kansas City Star*. She approached *The Star* in 1980 and suggested reviving their tradition of publishing original quilt blocks. *The Star* took her up on it in 2000. Her first series of original blocks, *Prairie Flower: A Year on the Plains*, appeared in *The Star* in 2001, her second, *Women of Design: Quilts in the Newspaper*, in 2004.

Hers is a name well-known in the quilt world, as she has written, lectured and taught about quilt history.

There are no quilters in her family tree. "We didn't have anything like that in my family," she said, but quilts have long had a hold on her. She remembers a childhood friend's pocket quilt, her college friends' bed quilts. When it came time for her college senior project for art education, she made a quilt.

"It was a really bizarre quilt. I got the Carrie Hall book and found a star and I made it. I cut triangles and squares and put it together—no templates. I made it out of clothes. Some were polyester. I quilted it with six-strand embroidery thread. It was horribly erratic. My professors rejected it."

She didn't give up. She thought a quilt would be perfect for her sister's wedding gift and tried again.

"My first quilts look like the haphazard rural quilts of the mid 20th century, which I guess they were. I've used them in my lectures to illustrate that style, made by a person in 1966 without any training."

By the time she made her fourth quilt, she had befriended some quilters. This quilt had templates and one-quarter inch seam allowances.

"There's something in me that makes me love patterns."

"I started out as an impulsive folk artist with no skills and over the years I've gone the other way," she said.

She also allows that quilts have sustained her through some difficult times.

"Life is hard. When your mother dies or you get divorced, you make quilts," she said.

Her start as a chronicler of quilt patterns came when she opened a drawer.

In an art history classroom at University of Kansas, she found blocks from the Carrie Hall collection, bequeathed to the university years before, stored in map drawers. She played with them. In 1967, she started categorizing them on index cards. She did that as a hobby until she had a box full of cards in 1979.

To share the information with others, she started typing out her categories with hand-drawn sketches and made photocopies. For years, it was her self-published first book. Today, it is the quilt resource book we all know, the "Encyclopedia of Pieced Patterns," published by the American Quilter's Society.

"There's something in me that makes me love patterns. I love and I'm really good at looking at disparate elements and putting them together," she said. "I have a very good visual memory. I remember patterns."

She was a founding member of the American Quilt Study Group. At their conventions, she met others who shared her interest in quilt blocks and patterns: Merikay Waldvogel, Joyce Gross, Cuesta Benberry. She and Merikay call themselves the Ob-Comp (obsessive-compulsive) pattern collectors.

Quilting was her hobby: her day job was as a special education teacher. She stopped teaching in 1982, then worked part-time conducting teacher training. She made the transition to full-time quilt work—writing, teaching, lecturing, curating exhibits—in 1985.

She's never looked back. She realizes her strengths: categorizing, sorting skills and a strong memory. "I'm like a human Xerox machine," she admits.

Being analytical hasn't hurt either. She decided people wanted to know more about fabric and made a conscious decision to shift from patterns to fabric. Her book *Clues in the Calico* was the result.

She's forged strong relationships with collaborators. She designs fabric with fellow quilt historian, Terry Thompson. She publishes patterns with fellow quilter, Karla Menaugh. She collaborates on books with her sister, acclaimed domestic dog scientist, Jane Brackman. She meets weekly with three lively quilt groups and is an active member of the Kaw Valley Quilter's Guild.

She lives in a Victorian cottage, filled with quilts and antiques. She's been there 30 years and declares she is married to her house.

Barbara will admit to having a great deal of energy and thinks her interest in quilting is a good way to channel it. "I could be stalking David Letterman and that's a waste of time."

*Barbara and her mother in New York City.*

# Aeroplane

Quilt size: 47" x 56" • Block size: 7 1/2" square

*Pieced by Pamela Mayfield, machine quilted by Lori Kukuk*
*In the collection of Kolbey Lee Huneycutt*

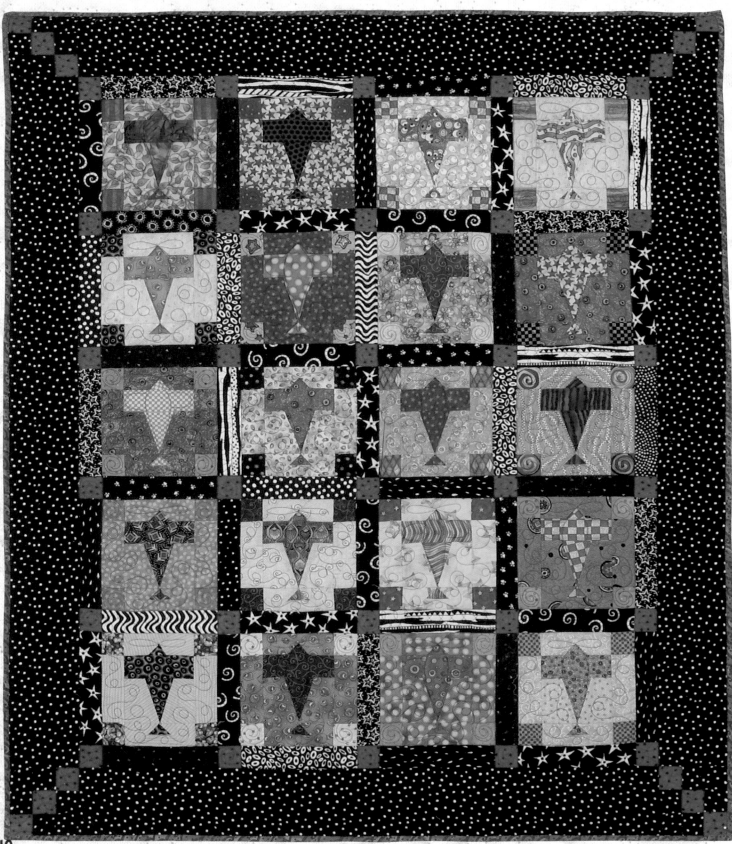

*C*harles Lindbergh's 1927 solo flight across the Atlantic inspired many a dream —and many a quilt. This design was published as "Aeroplane" on the "Good Cheer" page of the Oklahoma Farmer Stockman sometime in 1929. Patterns often appeared in more than one newspaper column. It was published in The Kansas City Star in July, 1929, as "The Aircraft Quilt" mailed in by reader, Mrs. Otto Prell, Miami, Oklahoma, who may have clipped it from one paper and mailed it to another.

Barbara designed this baby quilt and Pam stitched it in today's bright prints. The pattern here is modified with no set-in seams, so it is easier to piece than the original. We give you instructions for three methods: 1) patterns for piecing the design over paper foundations; 2) templates for traditional piecing; 3) instructions for rotary cutting those pieces.

## You'll need:

- 20 pieced blocks finishing to 7 1/2" square
- Sashing strips 1 1/2" x 8" and cornerstones 1 1/2" square
- Border 4 1/2" wide
- 4 corner blocks 4 1/2"

## Fabric requirements

### Blocks

Use quarter-yard pieces of brights for the blocks (either fat quarters or long quarters.)

Pam used small pieces from her terrific collection of bright prints, but you can get a similar effect by using the following:

- 3 lime greens
- 3 yellows
- 3 bright blues (buy an extra 1/2 yard of one for the binding)
- 3 oranges
- 3 reds
- 2 purples
- 1 pink

### Sashing

- 1/4 yard of red dot for the cornerstones.
- 6 fat quarters of black and white prints for the sashing rectangles will give you a variety. If you want to use just one print, you'll need 1 yard.

### Border

- 1 1/3 yards of black dot for the border.

### Backing

- 2 yards of black and white print to piece together a backing.

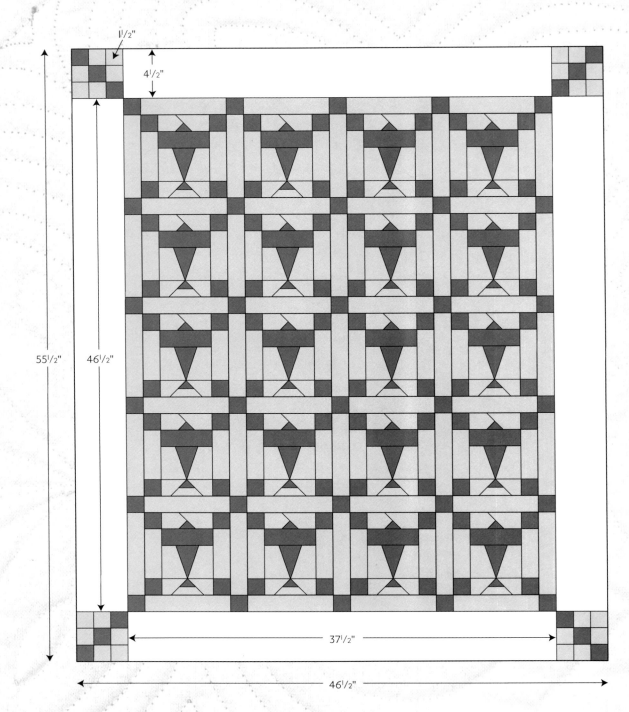

**1/2"**

**4¹/₂"**

**55¹/₂"**

**46¹/₂"**

**37¹/₂"**

**46¹/₂"**

QUILT DIAGRAM

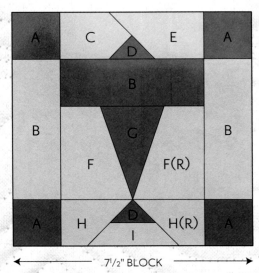

7¹/₂" BLOCK

# CUTTING

## BLOCKS

Decide which method you are going to use to piece the airplanes. If you want to paper-piece over a foundation, you won't need to cut any airplane pattern pieces beforehand. If you want to use conventional piecing methods, cut the pieces for 20 blocks as indicated on the templates.

### SASHING

- ❧ Cut 30 red 2" squares for the cornerstones.
- ❧ Cut 55 rectangles 2" x 8" of various black prints for the sashing strips.

### BORDER

- ❧ Cut 2 strips 5" x 47" for the side borders from the black dot.
- ❧ Cut 2 strips 5" x 38" for the top and bottom borders from the black dot.
- ❧ Cut 4 nine-patch blocks for the corners by cutting the following:
  24 squares 2" each from the black border fabric.
  16 squares 2" each from the red fabric.

## STITCHING THE BLOCKS
## TRADITIONAL PIECING

Piece the airplane blocks as shown below:

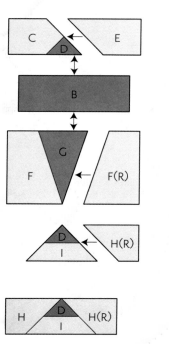
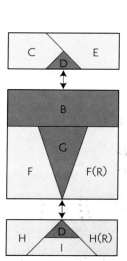
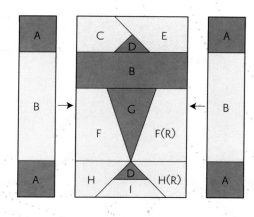
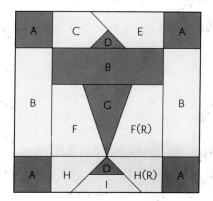

C
Cut I light

E
Cut I light

TEMPLATES FOR TRADITIONAL PIECING

A
Cut 4 dark
Rotary cut 2"
square

F & F(R)
Cut I light, flip
pattern and
cut I more

G
Cut I dark

B
Cut I dark
and 2 light
Rotary cut 2"x 5"
rectangles

H & H(R)
Cut I light, flip
pattern and
cut I more

D
Cut 2 dark

I
Cut I light

14

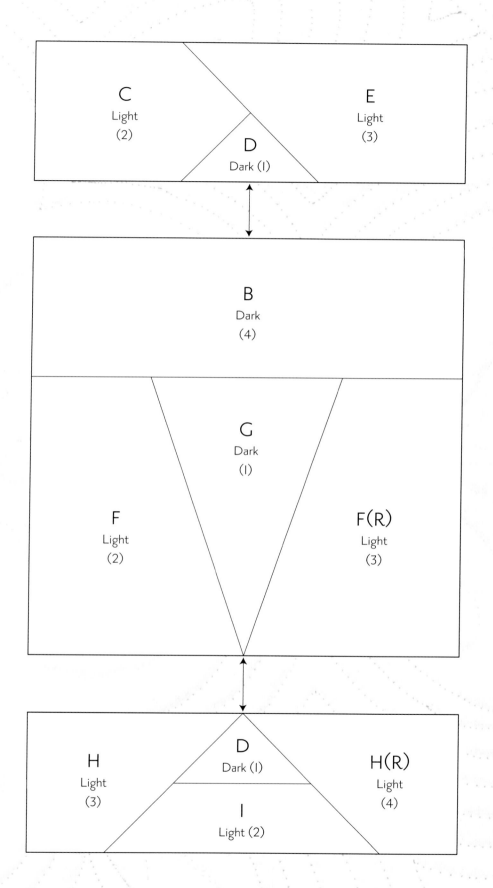

Paper-piece the airplane itself over these foundations.

[Note we give you permission to photocopy this page for your own personal use]

## PIECING THE AIRPLANES OVER PAPER FOUNDATIONS

* Photocopy the pattern 20 times on lightweight paper. (Note: we give you permission to copy page 15 for your personal use.)
* There are three parts to each airplane: the nose, the tail and the body with wing. Piece each separately.
* Follow the numbering order on the patterns.
* Before you remove the paper, sew the blocks together.
* Cut the left and right sides of each block by rotary cutting the following pieces

    Piece A: Cut 4 squares 2" each of a dark print.

    Piece B: Cut 2 rectangles 2" x 5" of the airplane's print.
* Piece two side strips and add them to the paper-pieced plane.
* Remove the paper.

## PIECING THE CORNER NINE PATCHES

Using conventional piecing methods, stitch together the squares as shown below:

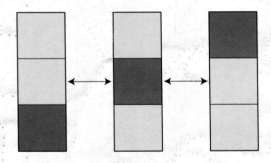

## SETTING THE QUILT

🍂 Press the blocks and trim the edges to make unfinished airplane blocks 8" square.

🍂 Add black sashing rectangles between the blocks, as shown below, making 5 strips of 4 blocks each.

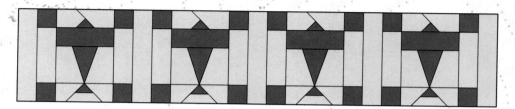

🍂 Stitch together alternating red squares and black rectangles to make the horizontal sashing, as shown below. Make 6 strips of 5 red squares and 4 black rectangles.

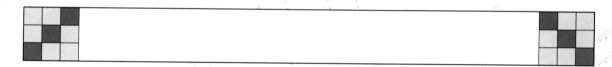

🍂 Set the blocks between the strips as shown in the quilt diagram.

🍂 Press the quilt top and trim edges if necessary.

🍂 Add the side border strips—the longer strips.

🍂 Piece the 4 pressed and trimmed "Nine-Patch" blocks to the shorter border strips, making sure the red squares line up as shown in the photo.

🍂 Attach the top and bottom borders.

🍂 Press the top and trim the edges, if necessary.

## QUILTING

Lori Kukuk did an imaginative job of machine-quilting this piece by stitching propellers on the noses of the planes and meandering an all-over pattern of loop-de-loops with a little spiral in each corner square. Hand quilters might want to stitch a propeller and then echo-quilt the shape of the plane. A traditional chain pattern—the single chain so popular in the mid-20th century—would make a good border design.

## MACHINE QUILTING SUGGESTIONS

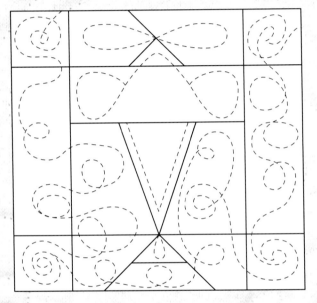

## HAND QUILTING SUGGESTIONS

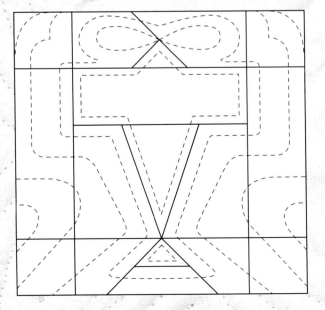

A cable for a 4-1/2" border

20

*"I love to teach."*

# Jane Buckley

Jane Buckley turned her energy from the business world to the quilting world in 1994. Since then, she maintained a busy schedule, working with quilt guilds and teaching quilters throughout this region. A self-described extrovert, she loves people. She enjoys the reaction she gets from an audience.

"When they start laughing, I think, ah, we're together now," she said.

Teaching quilting brings Jane's career full circle. Her first job was teaching home economics in a small West Virginia school. Her classroom doubled as the cafeteria for grades kindergarten through 12. She was in charge of the cafeteria too. Her home ec room was equipped with six treadle sewing machines. She and her husband, Tom, bought kits at Sears and motorized those machines.

Life lessons have taught Jane about teaching. She credits her minister father with being creative in getting the best out of people. "He loved working with people," she said. She credits her mother with teaching her handwork such as

sewing and knitting as a child. "They were both very patient parents," she remembers.

Her father gave Jane this advice about training people: "Teach your managers. Let them teach the other people."

Other valuable teaching training came from school days. "The best training I ever got was in the eighth grade. Every Friday we had to get up and give a two minute talk in front of the class," she said.

While growing up, "Mom always had us sewing or knitting," Jane said. She doesn't remember her mother quilting, but she does have two small baby quilts she made: one for Jane and one for Jane's daughter. Her father's artistic outlet was making wooden duck decoys.

Jane took her first quilting class in 1979.

> ## "I like to help students regain their sense of 'I can do this.'"

Virginia Robertson was her first teacher. Jane gained confidence about color in a sampler class. "There aren't a lot of different colors in a sampler, but I learned a lot," Jane said. She had things to re-learn from her background in home economics: "You didn't put purples and pinks together."

Jane has taken quilting classes ever since. "You can never stop learning."

She studied Libby Lehman's thread work in Houston. Others she has studied with include Virginia Anthony in Wichita, Jinny Beyer, Alex Anderson, Cheryl Phillips and many more, both local and national teachers.

"Different classes have made a great impact on me. If you're open and willing, you're going to learn something in every one of them," she said.

Another influential teacher was Linda Fielder, who taught her thread painting. "Learning thread painting has enhanced my work," Jane said.

A recent class with Sally Collins, "Detail with a Feather" has also influenced Jane's work. "She makes tiny quilts and she makes it easy. Being accurate is important. I picked up the 1/8" border idea from her," Jane said.

Along the way, she's developed relationships with many quilting friends. "The fun thing is how all of this hangs together. Our friendship makes a cloth," she said.

Jane's recent work has been influenced by strips and curves, as taught by Louisa Smith. She's now working on a color series of strips and curves quilts.

She blends techniques she learns in classes with her enjoyment of working with color.

"I like to use a lot of color," she said. "Many quilters garden but the green thumb went by me. I think that's why my quilts are so bright. I garden in my fabric."

Jane believes sewing fills a creative need for many people. "I think it's there in everybody," she said.

She's doing a lot of teaching now, more than she would like. She plans to cut back to teaching once a month. She suffered a heart attack in late 2002, but it barely slowed her down. Six weeks later, she was on a quilting tour to Australia and New Zealand.

The satisfaction teaching brings her is clear. "I like to see students come in looking apprehensive of the class and leave with the confidence that they can create something that's different," she said.

Confidence building is also a reward. She notices that women, "lose that self-confidence and enthusiasm at some point in life. I like to help students regain their sense of 'I can do this,' then see them relax and enjoy themselves."

"To build people's self confidence is one of the greatest pleasures of teaching," she said.

*Jane and Tom on their honeymoon, 1953*

# How Many Frogs are in the Forest?

*Stitched and quilted by Jane Buckley*

Size: 71" x 80"

How Many Frogs are in the Forest?

*M*ake a pillow, a wall hanging or a quilt. The instructions for making each follow. Jane describes how to piece, add batting and backing, then quilt as your work progresses. You'll have a reversible quilt when you are finished. Her focal fabric has little frogs peeking out from behind the wildlife, hence the name of her quilt.

## YOU'LL NEED:

- Basic sewing supplies: rotary cutter, 6" x 12" ruler and 12" square ruler, needles, etc.
- Batting (of high cotton content)
- Thread (bobbin thread should blend well with the backing/base fabric)
- Walking foot for sewing machine

## FABRIC REQUIREMENTS

100% cotton, pre-washed and ironed. Feel free to experiment with other fabrics, ribbons, etc. if desired. The pillow uses a muslin base, but larger projects use the quilt backing as the base for each pieced block.

- A focal fabric: choose one "conversation" print to be the focal fabric: animal prints, large flowers, seasonal prints, holiday prints, toys, people, fish, etc.
- Coordinating strips for blocks: strips of coordinating fabrics—lights, mediums, darks and brights—in a variety of colors that go well with the focal fabric. These can be any width, preferably wider than 1". Scraps and left-over strips from other projects work well. A variety of fabrics (8 or more) make your project more interesting. Solids do not work as well as multi-colors and prints.
- Two coordinating fabrics for seam-covering strips—one that matches the front of the quilt and one that matches the back.
- Two coordinating fabrics for reversible binding—one that matches the front of the quilt and one that matches the back.
- Backing (larger than the block size desired).

## FOR PILLOW

- Lightweight muslin base cut either 10" x 10" - 12" x 12" - or 14" x 14".
- Backing for pillow same size as muslin base plus 4".
- Bag of fiberfill for stuffing pillow or pillow form slightly smaller than the base size.

## FOR WALL HANGING OR QUILT

- Decide on the block size - for example, a 12" block.
- For a 3 block by 3 block wall hanging, prepare 9 pieces of batting and 9 pieces of backing fabric, each cut 2" wider than the block size desired.
- Cut the 2 fabrics for seam-covering strips into 1 1/4" wide strips. The amount of strips needed depends on the size and number of blocks you want to make.
- Cut strips for reversible binding. Cut 1 1/4" wide strips for the front binding and 1 3/4" strips for the back binding.

(Note: you might want to select different fabrics for each of these strips or use the same fabrics for all.)

## DIRECTIONS

❧ From the focal fabric, cut a pleasing shape with 3, 4 or 5 sides (depending on the size of the focal fabric motif). The sides of this center need not be parallel with each other.

❧ Cut fabric strips of varied widths, ranging from 1" - 2". These can be cut in straight or wedge shapes.

❧ Position the focal fabric. For the wall hanging and the quilt, layer backing, batting, then focus fabric on top. For the pillow, pin the focal fabric to muslin. Center the focal fabric as you like.

❧ Lay the first strip on one edge of focal fabric—right sides together—and stitch a 1/4" seam.

❧ Finger press strip open. Trim ends of strip even with the cut edge of the focal fabric.

❧ Add strips around the motif until you reach the outside edge of the block (see photo).

❧ Try to have a balance of color, but remember—there are no rights or wrongs for this method of construction.

❧ Press the completed block.

❧ Any decorative stitching or free motion quilting can be done now.

❧ Press and trim the block to the desired size.

## FINISHING THE PILLOW

🍂 Cut the backing a little larger than the pillow front. Ease the seam when sewing it together — right sides together — so you'll have room for stuffing or pillow form insertion. Trim corners. Turn right side out. Stuff/insert pillow form. Whip stitch opening together.

## FINISHING THE WALL HANGING/QUILT

### JOINING THE BLOCKS

🍂 Arrange the blocks as you please.

🍂 Add the batting and backing for each block. Quilt.

🍂 As you sew the blocks together, you will cover the seams—on both the front and back of the quilt—with seam-covering strips.

🍂 From the seam-covering fabric, cut 1 1/4" wide strips. Cut the strips to the size of the block. (Example: if block is 12", cut strips 1 1/4" by 12".) Cut strips for the front and the back of the quilt.

🍂 Place the front seam-covering strip along the side of the block front, right sides together. Line up the back seam-covering strip on the back at the same time, with the right sides facing. Pin as needed. Stitch, using a 1/4" seam. A walking foot is very helpful here.

🍂 Stay stitch 1/4" around the other 3 sides of the block to prevent stretching as you assemble the rows.

🍂 Sew the blocks together in rows. To stitch the blocks together, butt one edge of a block to another. Do not overlap the blocks. Be sure to keep blocks lined up so they don't stretch. Stitch the block edges together, using a wide and fairly short zigzag stitch over the butted edges. Repeat the zigzag stitching on the reverse side of the blocks. This ensures you've caught all the edges and adds stability to your quilt.

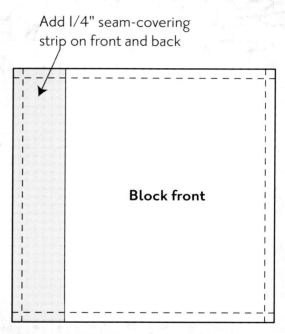

Add 1/4" seam-covering strip on front and back

**Block front**

- - - - - - - = stitching lines

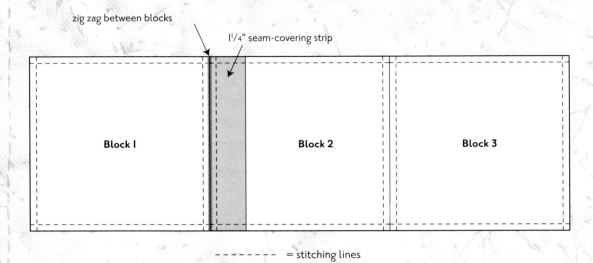

zig zag between blocks

1¹/4" seam-covering strip

Block 1

Block 2

Block 3

- - - - - - - - = stitching lines

❦ When each row of blocks is zigzagged together, complete the stitching on the seam-covering strips. Do the back first. Press the seam-covering strips open. Then press under a 1/4" seam on each strip and stitch it down. This can be done by hand or by using tiny zigzag stitches with matching or invisible thread. You can also do this using the blind hem stitch on your machine.

❦ Next, work on the front side of the quilt. Press the front seam-covering strips open. Press under 1/4" seam allowance on the raw edges. Finish by hand stitching the strip to the next block. The front seam-covering strips will hide the stitches from the back of the quilt. You'll have a reversible quilt when you are finished.

❦ To join the rows of blocks, prepare seam-covering strips as described above. For example, if the blocks are 12" square and you have positioned them in a 3 x 3 setting, you have 3 rows of 12" blocks, so your seam-covering strips need to be 1 1/4" by 36". You will only need a total of 2 strips in this example, because binding will cover the outer edges of your quilt.

❦ Use care when putting the rows together. Don't allow them to stretch and you'll have a perfect grid.

### R E V E R S I B L E   B I N D I N G :

Using 1 1/4" strips for front binding fabric and 1 3/4" strips of back binding fabric, make reversible binding in the following way.

❀ Press the back binding strip in half, wrong sides together so you have a strip about 7/8" wide. Line up the edges of the 1 1/4" wide front binding with this back binding, right sides together and stitch using a 1/4" seam. Press open.

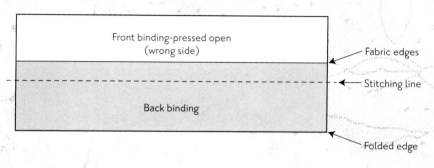

Front binding-pressed open
(wrong side)

— Fabric edges

- — Stitching line

Back binding

— Folded edge

❀ Make enough of this binding for each side of the quilt, plus 1". Position the front binding, right sides together, 1/4" away from cut edge of the quilt front. Extend the ends of the strip 1/2" beyond top and bottom edges of quilt. Stitch.

❀ When turned, the seam of the two binding fabrics will line up exactly at the edge of the quilt. Turn binding to the quilt back and blind hem stitch in place by hand.

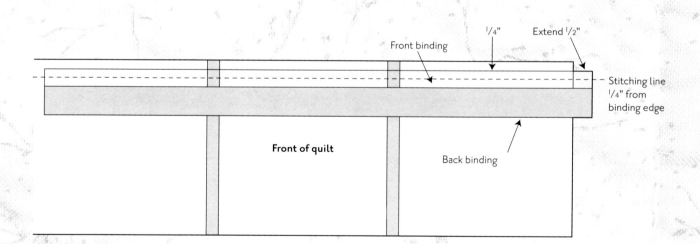

1/4"    Extend 1/2"

Front binding

Stitching line
1/4" from
binding edge

Front of quilt

Back binding

❀ Once the quilt sides are bound, finish the top and bottom in the same way.

❀ Turn in the 1/2" extensions at the corners, clipping as needed and whip stitch edges together.

❀ Label and date your quilt.

—Jane Buckley, 2005

*If you talk with Rosemary Cromer long enough about quilting, she will fix you with a determined look and explain its importance to her:*
*"I must do this. I think it's your soul."*

# Rosemary Cromer

It's her time now, time to explore color and creativity and revel in the experience. Her three kids are grown. She taught countless students in middle school and junior college classes.

Retirement three years ago turned her loose from those responsibilities. A battle with cancer was in full swing then. She won and she's celebrating daily.

Color is her passion. "I used to be so safe but as I age, I throw the safety away," she said.

Quilting is something this former home economics teacher has done for a long time. She noticed resurgence in quilting during the nation's bicentennial celebration in 1976 and took it up in 1977 "when I was through with tiny babies," she said. She began by taking a sampler class from Rosie Grinstead in Overland Park.

Sewing was something she learned growing up in Bronson, Kansas. Her mother's sense of style was an enduring influence.

"I grew up in a household that didn't hurry a lot. We went through the day's work trying new things and appreciating beauty," she said. "My mother planted flowers to use in arrangements in our house and at the church. She made her own clothes and gave herself perms and maintained her own sense of style. I cannot remember a single day when our beds were not made—except when the sheets were drying on the line. She was always sewing in her spare time and clipping ideas from magazines and newspapers."

31

Retirement brought a return to that unhurried lifestyle. She decided to explore Kansas City's Country Club Plaza, with camera in hand. She photographed designs she noticed on buildings there and worked with graph paper and ruler to arrange those design elements into a quilt. Tile designs, a wavy Brush Creek and grain from the Board of Trade building all found their way into her Plaza quilt.

In the meantime, a home economics colleague talked her into teaching quilting at a local quilt shop. The shop's owner noticed her working on a Plaza block and encouraged her to make it into a pattern. She also offered her a part-time job at the shop. Time there is a break from her "studio time"—time spent designing and stitching her quilt tops.

She challenges herself and sets goals for her work.

She learned all she could about paper-foundation piecing and made a queen-size quilt using that method. Another quilt, "The Spirit of New Zealand," was selected to compete in the juried American Quilter's Society's 2004 Quilt Show in Paducah, Kentucky. Its design was a colorful mystery quilt pattern from *New Zealand Quilter* magazine.

> ## "Aging and the crises in our lives build the basis for our creativity."

New challenges include learning the ins and outs of a new electronic sewing machine, which will consume some months of study. She speaks to quilt groups about creativity, a topic close to her heart.

Her lecture celebrates achievements of people in their golden years.

"Aging and the crises in our lives build the basis for our creativity," she says. She also thinks that a lack of inhibition that often comes with getting older helps.

She finds the talk evokes emotions and even moves some listeners to tears. "It gives people hope. They say maybe I do have something left."

Since leaving her more hectic life as a foods teacher behind, she finds that her own journey into the creative process often feels like moving into the unknown. She's found ideas need time to evolve and that it's important to focus on the moment in front of you. Besides time, she seeks solitude, space to work, continual learning, encouragement, independence and connecting with nature and the arts.

She also finds it important to surround yourself with those who lift you up.

"My parents provided this setting in my childhood and allowed my passion a chance to develop," she said. "Now my husband and family provide that setting. I consciously work to keep everything in balance. I share this when I talk to quilt groups so other quilters can define ways to nurture their own creativity and that of their friends."

*Rosemary, age 1, with brother Allen*

## More about Rosemary ...

❀ Born: May 6, 1945, Fort Scott Hospital, Kansas. Parents: Reuben Warren, rural mail carrier, and Alice Warren, homemaker and independent insurance agent.

❀ Became interested in sewing: at age 8 in 4-H in hometown of Bronson, Kansas.

❀ Married: high-school sweetheart Joe Cromer 1969. Three children: Alisha, Joe Allen and Nicole.

❀ Influenced by: teachers who "led me to believe that I could do anything"—Vivian Bartlett, Eula Lewis, Ruth Butts, Mary Hankammer; quilters Rosie Grinstead, and Aunt Willa Jakway and the Bronson Methodist Quilters; Elaine Johnson.

❀ Education: BS in Family & Consumer Science Ed., Pittsburg State University; MS in FACS Ed., Kansas State University.

❀ Other accomplishments: her quilt "The Spirit of New Zealand" was selected for juried American Quilter's Society Quilt Show and Contest in Paducah, KY, April 2004.

❀ Teaches: "If the Shoe Doesn't Fit, Then Go Barefoot," a class about creativity.

❀ Guild membership: Quilter's Guild of Greater Kansas City since 1995.

# Fiesta

Size: 13" x 30"

Left: Stitched and quilted by Rosemary Cromer
Right: Stitched and quilted by Judy Wenger

*The colors in this table runner were inspired by Rosemary's collection of colorful Fiesta dishes. She originally learned to paper-piece for a quilt project that grew so large, it's now on her bed. Rosemary adapted that design to create this original table runner. Her friend, Judy Wenger, made her table runner in the colors of the Christmas season. Here are instructions describing how to paper-piece this project:*

## You'll need:

- Basic sewing supplies: rotary cutter, 6" x 12" ruler and 12" square ruler, needles, etc.
- Batting (of high cotton content)
- Thread (bobbin thread should blend well with the backing/base fabric)
- Walking foot for sewing machine

## Fabric needed (6 total)

- Fat quarters of three fabrics (A, C, and D)
- 1/8 yard of one fabric (E)
- 2/3 yard of one fabric (includes binding) (B)
- 1/2 yard of one fabric (includes backing) (F)

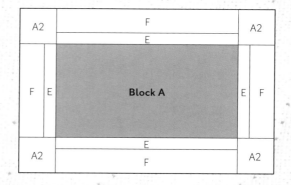

## Block A
### Cut

For paper-piecing:
- A1: 1 - 3" x 7 1/2" (for center)
- B, C and D: 1 - 2" x 44" strip

For piecing to complete block A:
- A2: 4 - 3 3/4" squares (for corner blocks)
- E: 1 - 1 1/2" x 44" strip
- F: 1 - 2 3/4" x 44" strip

### Sew

- Piece fabrics A-D together in numbered order shown on Block A (1-13). Trim edges.
- For outer border, stitch E to F. Cut 2 – 11 1/2" strips and 2 – 6 3/4" strips.
- Stitch the longer strips to the longer block edges.
- Stitch A2 corner block to each end of the shorter strips. Stitch to block sides.
- Trim block to measure 13 1/4" x 17 3/4".

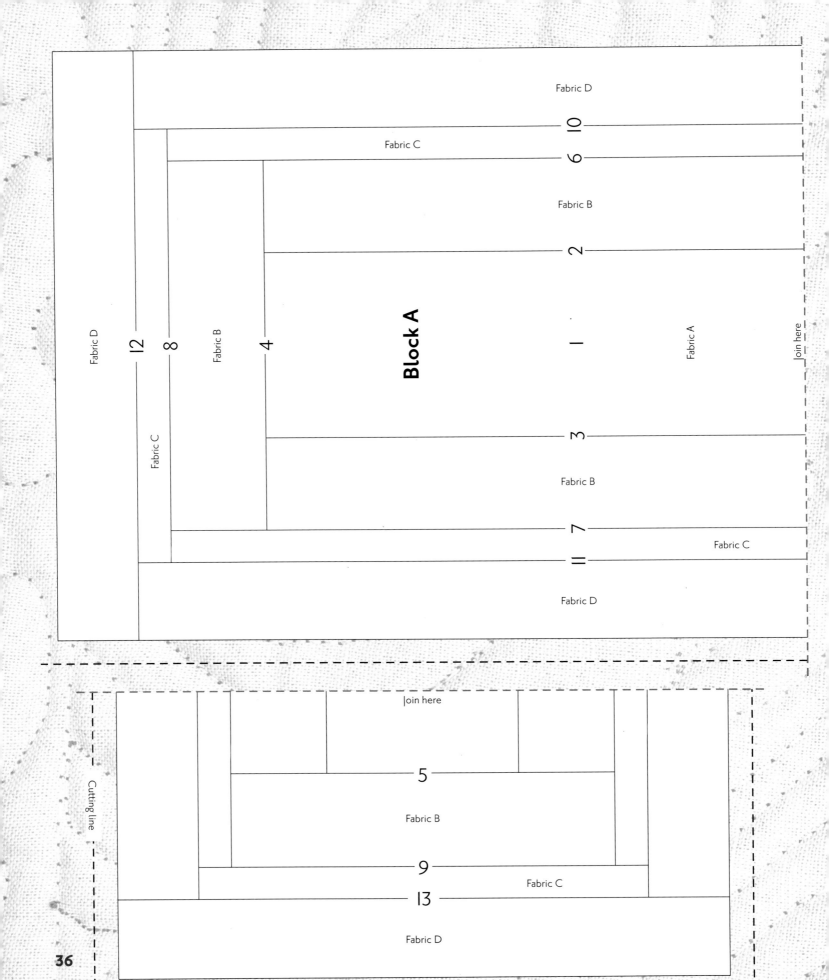

Fabric D

Fabric C

10

6

Fabric B

2

Block A

Fabric D

12

8

Fabric B

4

1

Fabric A

Fabric C

Join here

3

Fabric B

7

Fabric C

11

Fabric D

Join here

Cutting line

5

Fabric B

9

Fabric C

13

Fabric D

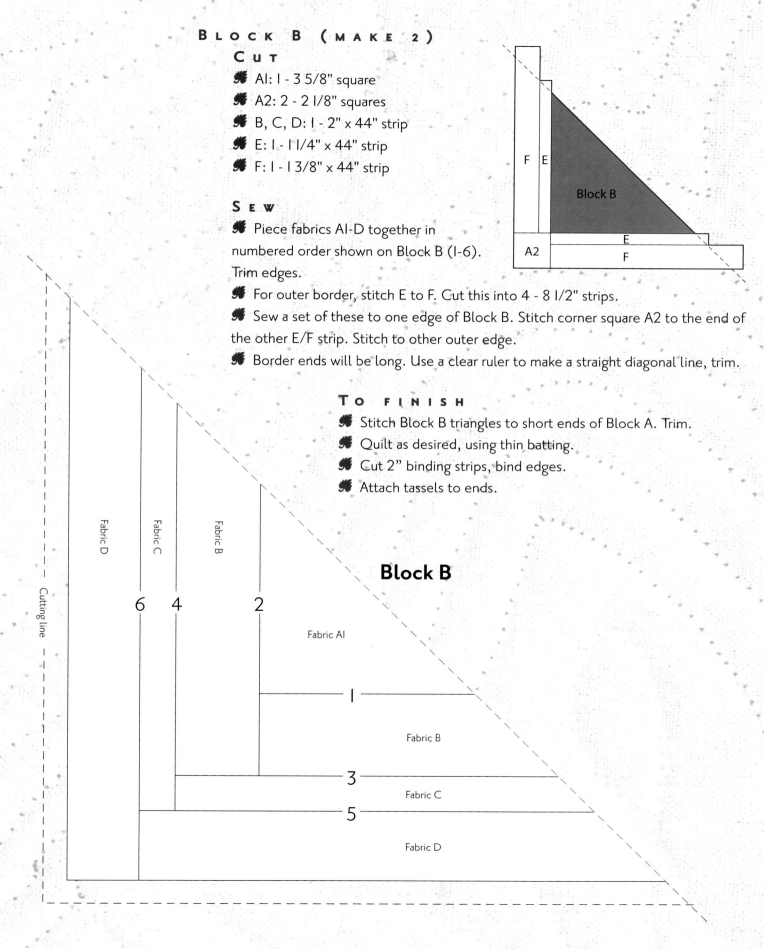

## Block B (make 2)

### Cut

- ❧ A1: 1 - 3 5/8" square
- ❧ A2: 2 - 2 1/8" squares
- ❧ B, C, D: 1 - 2" x 44" strip
- ❧ E: 1 - 1 1/4" x 44" strip
- ❧ F: 1 - 1 3/8" x 44" strip

### Sew

- ❧ Piece fabrics A1-D together in numbered order shown on Block B (1-6). Trim edges.
- ❧ For outer border, stitch E to F. Cut this into 4 - 8 1/2" strips.
- ❧ Sew a set of these to one edge of Block B. Stitch corner square A2 to the end of the other E/F strip. Stitch to other outer edge.
- ❧ Border ends will be long. Use a clear ruler to make a straight diagonal line, trim.

### To finish

- ❧ Stitch Block B triangles to short ends of Block A. Trim.
- ❧ Quilt as desired, using thin batting.
- ❧ Cut 2" binding strips, bind edges.
- ❧ Attach tassels to ends.

Block B

F  E

Block B

E

A2

E

F

Cutting line

Fabric D

Fabric C

Fabric B

6   4   2

Fabric A1

1

Fabric B

3

Fabric C

5

Fabric D

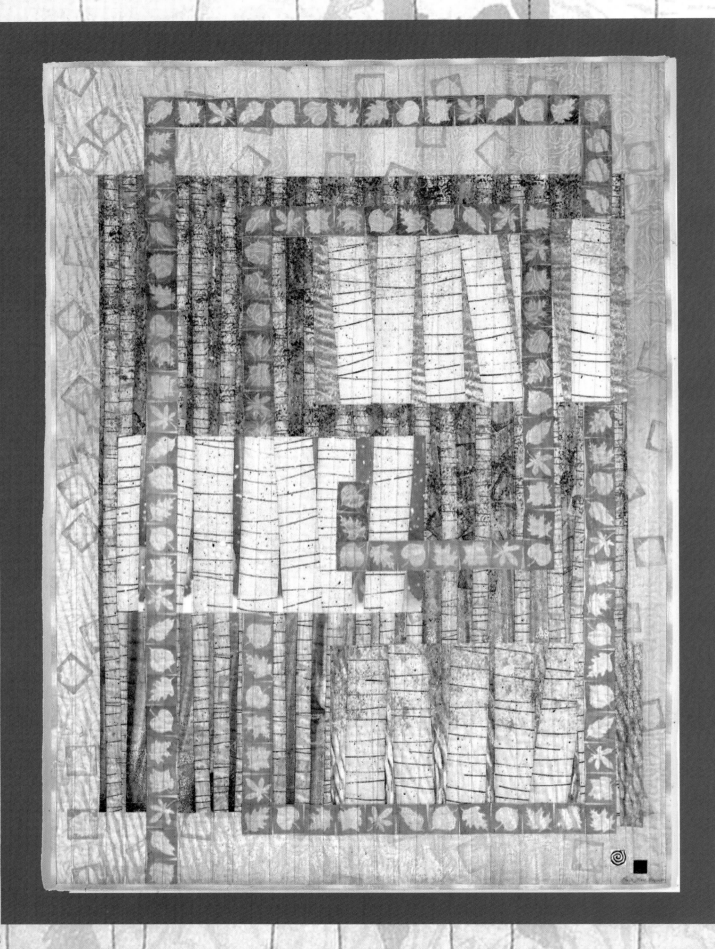

*Chris Wolf Edmonds is not the first artist to grace her family tree.*

# Chris Wolf Edmonds

In 1881, her great grandfather, Severin John Keimig, emigrated from Germany to homestead on the Kansas prairie near Zenda. More an artist than a farmer at heart, he stretched canvas from floor to ceiling and painted architectural columns, flora and fauna on the interior walls of the home he shared with his wife and eight children.

The art of other family members inspired her as well.

In his free time, Chris's father inlaid wood and carved lovely songbirds and ducks, some of which grace her mantle today. She uses the woodworking skills she learned from him to carve wood-blocks to use when printing her fabric.

From her mother, she learned to value the creativity of fine sewing. Her mother stitched dresses and coats for Chris and her two younger sisters, as well as teaching them a wide variety of needle arts. Her grandmother, a professional seamstress, sewed in her home for her family as well as others.

"My admiration for them and the beautiful and useful things they created with their hands led me to quiltmaking," she said. One of her warmest memories is pulling fabrics and quilt blocks out of closets and trunks at her grandmother's house, spreading them on the floor or bed and planning new patterns. "My grandmother always encouraged me to sew and appreciated my creative approach."

Chris started her first quilt in 1963 while she was in college. It was a big pieced bed quilt, finished years later. She studied magazine articles and looked for books on how to make quilts. "There were only a few old

39

books available in the library then. With my background in sewing, I could handle pieced patterns but I wanted to do free-form things. I learned appliqué by trial and error," she said.

Early in her marriage, she set up a studio in the garage for wood-block printing, silk-screening and painting. But her knowledge of fabric kept her coming back to quiltmaking. "I've always made art, even in grade school," she said. "I enjoy the tactile, working with cloth. I came to that through my upbringing."

Her first original quilt designs were for babies. For her son born in 1969, there were "cross stitch animals on kettle cloth," she laughs. "It was sturdy!" *Quilter's Newsletter Magazine* published the patterns she had designed. Many will also remember her children's appliquéd barn quilt, featured by QNM in 1978.

> ## "I believe it is the nature of artists to manipulate the art of nature."

She was one of a group who worked on Lawrence's Bicentennial quilt. "Working on blocks for that quilt brought us together," she said. "We enjoyed each other's company and inspiration.

Some of the group attended the Nebraska Quilt Symposium in 1977 and were inspired to form the Kaw Valley Quilter's Guild with Chris as president. The following year, they worked with Kansas University to organize their own national symposium featuring Kansas quilts and quiltmakers, past and present.

As her quilts gained attention, Chris was invited to teach and lecture, eventually worldwide. Her quilts were included in many prestigious shows and collections and have been published in numerous books and magazines.

After 25 years of traveling, Chris now spends more time working in her home studio. "I was frustrated being away from home but I really enjoyed the friends I made."

Chris's talents have helped to move quilts into the art world during her lifetime. "In the late '70s, I realized that quiltmaking could be my vocation as well as my avocation," she said. "It was then that I began to approach my work more as an art form. In the early '80s, I began painting, dying and printing all of my own fabric."

Chris no longer enters many juried shows. She now exhibits and sells her work in one woman shows and featured artist gallery shows. "This is very comfortable for me, creating a body of work for about one show a year. It frees me to work at my own pace."

Painting fabric remains her favorite work. "I collect the colors and patterns of nature and attempt to preserve them in my work. I believe it is the nature of artists to manipulate the art of nature."

*Chris, age 2*

## MORE ABOUT CHRIS...

❧ Born: Feb. 17, 1943, in Wichita, Kansas. Parents: Betty Anderson Wolf, creative homemaker, and Lawrence Winton Wolf, small business owner.

❧ Married to Stephen Edmonds, June 11, 1966. Two children: Jason and Brynn.

❧ Influenced by: Impressionist painters; Bonnard, Monet, Van Gogh.

❧ Education: BS in Education, University of Kansas.

❧ Quilts published in: *American Craft, American Quilter, Fiber Arts, Good Housekeeping, Quilter's Newsletter Magazine, Smithsonian, The Art Quilt, 30 Distinguished Quilt Artists of the World.*

❧ Honors: Kansans of Distinction Award for Visual Arts, 2003; *Cherokee Trail of Tears* recognized as one of the 100 best American quilts of the 20th century, 1999. Between 1976 and 1999, her works earned: six Best of Show awards and two Judges Choice awards. Twelve were chosen for magazine covers.

❧ Favorite quote: "There are artists who transform the sun into a yellow spot, but there are others who with the help of their art and their intelligence transform a yellow spot into the sun." —Pablo Picasso

❧ Guild membership: Kaw Valley Quilter's Guild.

# Portrait of Trees: Summer/Winter

Size: 41" x 51"

*Stitched and quilted by Chris Wolf Edmonds*
*In the collection of the American Quilt Society Museum*

*T*he quilt at left is a good illustration of Chris's fabric painting technique, which is explained below. The quilt pictured on page 38 is Portraits of Trees: Four Seasons. It measures 39" x 54" and was also stitched and quilted by Chris. It is now in the collection of Emprise Bank. Both are part of her tree series, completed in 2000 and 2001.

As a teacher, I have always tried to provide my students with the tools to support their own creativity. I teach techniques such as dyeing, painting and printmaking. I encourage their use for original designs.

My first classes were in my home in the afternoon while my son was in kindergarten and my daughter was taking her nap. We sat around my dining room table. I taught how to make accurate templates, piecing, appliquéing and hand quilting.

The next year, I was invited to teach for "Textile Workshops of Kansas," a program sponsored by the Association of Community Arts Councils of Kansas and supported by the National Endowment for the Arts. Quiltmaking was enjoying a national rebirth, and from then on, invitations to teach and lecture began to pour in.

My most recent class was in Berlin, Germany. I taught color and design using fabric painting and printing techniques to an international class—through an interpreter. It was a far cry from an afternoon around my dining room table.

One thing that has not changed is the most important encouragement I give to my students: extend the art form, don't merely repeat it. Respect the tradition by advancing it.

## TO PRINT ON FABRIC YOU NEED:

- ❧ Print block
- ❧ Paint
- ❧ Paint pad
- ❧ Fabric

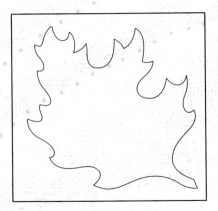

**Oak**

### PRINT BLOCK

Most of my print blocks are carved from wood, which can be washed and reused limitlessly. However, blocks may also be made of paper much more quickly and with simpler tools. If treated carefully, these may also be reused within limits. To make a paper print block, you will need the following supplies and tools, available at art, hobby or craft stores:

- 3/16" foam core (this comes in sheets like poster board, but with a thin layer of Styrofoam sandwiched in between two layers of paper)
- Xacto knife with #11 blade or Olfa art knife
- Sobo glue
- Cutting mat
- Carbon paper

Measure and cut a piece of foam core for the print block using your craft knife. Cut a second piece the same size to use as a supportive backing for the print block. Use a protective cutting mat to cover your work surface. Transfer the leaf design or a design of your own to the print block using carbon paper.

Following the design outline, cut straight down through the top layer of paper and into the foam core. Take care not to cut through the bottom layer of paper. Next, decide whether you want a positive or a negative image. You may cut away the area surrounding the design, leaving the positive image of the leaf to print. Or, you may cut away the leaf shape, leaving the surrounding area to print a negative image of the leaf.

Carefully cut away small areas at a time, removing the top layer of paper and picking out the foam beneath with the point of the knife. When the carving is complete, glue the print block to the supportive backing you cut earlier. Brush a layer of glue on the design side to seal all edges and surfaces. Cut a couple of small foam core squares and glue on the backing to serve as handles when you are printing.

## PAINT

- 🍂 fabric paint
- 🍂 iron

I use Createx (see source list at back of book) multi-surface acrylic colors. This paint is manufactured for use on fabric (and many other surfaces). It is soft, flexible, ready to use out of 8, 16 or 32 oz. plastic bottles, color-fast and washable. It is water based, making mixing and cleanup easy. The color can be heat-set by ironing at fabric settings for 2 minutes. It comes in a great array of colors (although I mix my own colors with 3 primary colors, black and white), as well as metallics, pearls, and iridescents.

Of course, there are other water-based fabric paints available from other companies. Don't be afraid to experiment and find what works best for you.

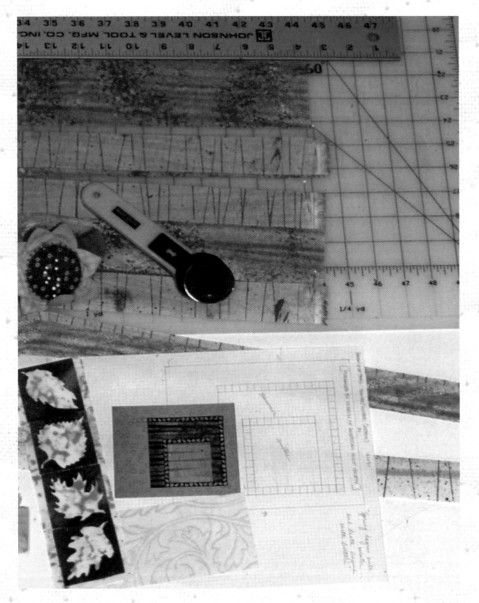

## PAINT PAD

❦ 1/4" foam rubber (may be purchased by the foot or yard from upholstery stores or fabric/craft stores)

❦ Plastic or waxed paper

❦ 1" putty knife

With scissors, cut a pad that is several times larger than the size of your print block. Paint will soak through the pad so you may want to place a piece of plastic or waxed paper under it. I have a formica-topped work table which is easily scrubbed clean with soap and water.

Once you have chosen or mixed your colors, you are ready to print. Keep a spray bottle of water handy to moisten the paint pad before you apply the paint and occasionally as you work. Use a palette knife or 1" putty knife to apply and smooth the paint into the pad, covering an area slightly larger than the size of the print block. More than one color may be applied for a multicolored effect.

Press the print block onto the paint pad 2 or 3 times to be sure all printing surfaces are coated with paint. You will need to reapply paint to the pad after printing your image a number of times or when you see it is no longer printing the complete image.

(Note: If you apply too much paint, your image will begin to fade and become transparent. If you do not use enough paint or water, the image will only partially print. Practice for a while until you learn to control all the elements to produce an image that meets your creative vision.)

## FABRIC

- ❦ 100% cotton fabric
- ❦ paper towels
- ❦ iron

If you buy fabric from the bolt in a fabric store, it will have sizing applied to the surface to give it a smooth, finished look. You will need to wash it to remove the sizing so that it will take the paint, and so that shrinkage will occur before you use it. You will also need to iron it if you want it to have a smooth surface for your painting and/or printing.

It is possible to buy unsized cotton print cloth by the bolt if you will be using a lot of it. I go through a 50-yard bolt about once a year. See the source list at the back of the book for information about my favorite, Testfabrics.

Before you print, cut your fabric into manageable pieces—one or two yards or even strips or blocks if you have a specific use in mind. Roll out two or three layers of soft paper toweling to cushion the fabric as you press the print block on it. Press down the block firmly, then remove carefully. Allow your printed fabric to dry and then set the color by ironing for 2 minutes on cotton setting.

Now you are ready to cut and sew...enjoy!

—Chris Wolf Edmonds, 2005

*Thanks to Nancy Hornback's curiosity, we know much more about Kansas quilts and quilt history.*

# Nancy Hornback

**H**er abiding interest in quilt research came about through her involvement in several projects in the mid 1980's.

She returned to college to begin work on her master's degree. She met quilters and together they began the Wichita quilt guild. She helped start the Kansas Quilt Project, a 3-year project to document quilts in Kansas. The project encompassed 72 quilt discovery days throughout the state. People in Kansas could bring in their quilts to be evaluated and documented.

Nancy's major was liberal studies, combining three areas of interest: women's studies, art history and social history. She wanted to interview women who had lived through the depression. A fellow quilter referred to that as getting their oral histories and Nancy said, "Oh, that's what you call it."

A project was born. The research Nancy began continues to this day.

A precursor to the Kansas Quilt Project was the Heartland Quilt Symposium in 1985. Antique quilts were shown at the symposium and quilt discovery days were conducted to find them. "It was very successful. About 150 quilts were documented in Wichita," Nancy said.

The quilt that captivated her at that symposium was a cherry basket quilt, made in 1870 by a 16-year-old girl. "That started a lot of things for me," she said. That quilt is now in the collection of the Wichita/Sedgwick County Historical Museum.

Nancy sewed as a little girl, did embroidery and made her own clothes in high school. Her mother taught her to sew as she grew up in the Imperial Valley, the desert of southern California.

49

There were plenty of pleasures in her childhood, especially playing outdoors for hours on end. "We hiked and climbed trees and played baseball," she said.

Quilts were not part of those days. "I never saw a quilt being made until I made one myself."

That happened after her mother died in 1973. Instead of dwelling on her grief, she decided to try to recapture childhood sewing memories by making a quilt. "I can sit around and feel sad or I can make a quilt."

Nancy was a full-time mother then. Her husband's career brought their growing family to Wichita. She pored over library books about quilts and started out ambitiously, making a red and yellow Lemoyne star bed quilt. It took two years. "I was so proud of it," she said.

Her next two quilts were made for her kids. One was made of blue jean patches and embroidered, another was an appliqué quilt. Both ideas came from magazines.

By 1982, her interest in quilting led her to be one of six founders of the Prairie Quilt Guild in Wichita.

Her next project, the Kansas Quilt Project, was the 11th such project in the country. Nancy and co-founder Eleanor Malone gathered information about how other states had conducted their projects. They put together a board that included historians, a home economist and quilters. In the fall of 1986, they had a try-out day to test the Quilt Discovery Day process.

> ## "I can sit around and feel sad or I can make a quilt."

"The fun was when a great quilt would come in. It was like Christmas. They'd start to unfold it and you didn't know what you were going to get," Nancy said. She also likened the interest to that in *Roots*, a popular book at that time, which encouraged people to explore their own family history.

"The Kansas Quilt Project got people interested in collecting the stories about people in their family who made these quilts," Nancy said.

Red and green quilts became her favorite. The topic also became her master's thesis project, culminating in a 1992 exhibit of 12 red and green antique appliqué quilts at the Wichita-Sedgwick County Historical Museum.

Tracking down quilting stories has consumed her time ever since.

One story involved Rachel Adella Jewett and Lucyle Jewett, a mother and daughter from Halstead, Kansas. Nancy and Sara Reimer Farley spent five years researching them and their quilting activities. Lucyle alone made 252 quilts, 34 of them rainbow star quilts which are made of diamond-shaped pieces that radiate from the center in concentric circles.

"They kept wonderful records about their work. The quilting was especially exquisite on their quilts," Nancy said. Lucyle was 100 years old when she passed away in 2000.

In the evening, she quilts for relaxation. All her quilts are hand appliquéd and hand quilted. She loves the process of handwork and has no doubt that making quilts by hand is right for her. "Lucyle said hand pieced quilts have a softer look to them. A machine stitched quilt does not lie on top of you in the same way."

"When my life is going off in so many directions, if I can sit and stitch for a while in the evening, I feel better. I sleep better. I feel calmer," she said.

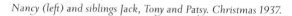

*Nancy (left) and siblings Jack, Tony and Patsy. Christmas 1937.*

## MORE ABOUT NANCY...

❦ Born: August 5, 1936, in El Centro, California. Parents: Arles Andrews Adams, flax mill superintendent and local authority on desert lore, and Jean Stewart Adams, stay-at-home mom.

❦ Became interested in sewing: my mother taught me to sew. By high school, I was making many of my clothes.

❦ Married: Terry Hornback, 1959. Seven children: Anne, John, Dave, Paul, Joe, Mary Elizabeth and Patrick.

❦ Influenced by: my parents.

❦ Education: B.A. in Sociology, University of San Diego, 1958; M.A. in Liberal Studies, Wichita State University, 1992.

❦ Published: several magazine articles, chapter entitled "Nineteenth-Century Red and Green Appliqué Quilts" in *Kansas Quilts and Quilters*, 1993.

❦ Other accomplishments: one of six founders of Prairie Quilt Guild of Wichita, 1982; co-founder, board member and Quilt Discovery Day Coordinator, Kansas Quilt Project, 1986-1993; board member, American Quilt Study Group, 1992-1999.

❦ Curated exhibits:
   • "Quilts in Red and Green," Wichita-Sedgwick County Historical Museum, 1992.
   • "Community Legacy: Quilts of Halstead, Kansas" (with Sara Reimer Farley), AQSG Seminar, Lawrence, 1997.
   • "Quilts Uncovered: AQSG Celebrates 20 Years of Quilt Scholarship," Paducah, Kentucky, 2000.

❦ Guild membership: Prairie Quilt Guild of Wichita, American Quilt Study Group.

# Cherry Baskets

Quilt size: 48" by 48"

Block size: 22" finished square

Hand appliquéd and hand quilted by Nancy Hornback

Border machine quilted by Lori Kukuk

Nancy Hornback drafted the pattern for this crib-sized quilt from a quilt that has a great deal of meaning to her, the masterpiece Cherry Baskets quilt stitched by Mary Parks Lawrence in 1870. Nancy first saw the quilt in 1985 and it inspired her study of red and green quilts. The original Cherry Baskets quilt is now in the collection of the Wichita Sedgwick County Historical Museum.

Mary Parks Lawrence was born near Auburn in Logan County, Kentucky, in 1854. She was a fifth-generation descendant of a Scots-Irish immigrant to Pennsylvania. Growing up on her family's tobacco plantation, Mary learned spinning, weaving and quilting skills and sewed garments for her father and brothers. Her father bought a sewing machine in exchange for Mary's promise to make coats for the family. When she was sixteen, Mary traded some of her handwoven goods for commercially manufactured fabrics to make her Cherry Baskets quilt. She hand-appliquéd the red, pink and orange pieces of her floral but used the machine to appliqué the leaves and stems. She also machine quilted a piano key design in the narrow white borders on the original quilt.

Mary came to Kansas with her parents in 1878 to homestead between Hunnewell and Drury in Sumner County. In 1881, she married William Lawrence, a cattleman and widower with five small children who lived on an adjoining farm. The Lawrences had four more children.

## To make this quilt:

### Fabric requirements

- 3 yards background fabric
- 1/2 yard green for stems/leaves
- 1/2 yard red for flower, baskets and cherries
- 1/4 yard orange for flowers, basket
- 1/4 yard pink for flowers, basket
- Embroidery floss for cherry stems

### Cutting and assembly

- Cut 2 1/2" strips of background fabric, enough for 4 borders. Set aside.
- Cut out four background pieces, 24" square. Trim backgrounds to 22 1/2" square after appliqué is complete.
- Cut out all pieces, adding seam allowances. Prepare for your usual appliqué style.
- Piece the two sides of the flower strips together in sections (see template). Add the bud, then join the two sides together.
- Piece the basket strips together. Add the basket top and handles.
- Arrange all pieces on the background block, following the pattern for placement. Pin or baste all in place.
- Appliqué.
- Embroider the cherry stems using a straight stitch.

### To finish

- When the appliqué is finished, stitch the blocks together.
- Add the border strips around the quilt.
- Add batting and backing, then quilt as desired. Bind.

Full Size
(add seam allowance)

Cherry Basket
(Center top)

Join A

Join B

54

Full Size
(add seam allowance and reverse all on other side)

Join A

Cherry Basket
(Corner top)

Join C

Join D

Full Size
(add seam allowance)

Cherry Basket
(Center bottom)

Join C

Join D

Chain Stitch

Cherry Basket
(Corner bottom)

Full Size
(add seam allowance and reverse all on other side)

57

Many will recognize Edie McGinnis as the most well-known quilter within the Kansas City Star's workforce.

# Edie McGinnis

**W**hen she went to work there in April of 1987, her voice was one of a chorus clamoring for *The Kansas City Star* to redraft and publish their massive collection of patterns.

Former publisher James Hale granted her permission to reprint patterns from *The Star*. She found her initial plan to redraft all the patterns into 12" squares "daunting." "My idea was to redraft the blocks, add seam allowances and rotary cutting instructions and get rid of the errors in them," she said.

Hale's fondness of quilting stemmed from sentimental memories of watching his mother quilt. He suggested Edie take her idea to another staffer, who dismissed her project with this proclamation: "Because of the great age of the ladies who quilt, there will never be enough interest in those old quilt patterns."

Edie estimates *The Star* quilt block collection numbers 1068 blocks, but feels certain there are still patterns to be discovered. Different editions of *The Star* published different patterns. *The Star* did not keep track of the patterns they had published. If one was interested in a particular pattern, one had to get it from Microfilm, which meant you needed to know what date the pattern was published.

On the 75th anniversary of the patterns first being published in *The Star*, Edie was interviewed about quilts for a story commemorating the occasion.

*The Star* started its book division in 2000. When casting about for publishing ideas, the quilt patterns were a book just waiting to happen.

The enterprise became a crash course in quilting for *Star* staffers. Edie's quilting knowledge was in demand. She showed the template artist how to make templates. She explained quilt techniques.

Some quilt patterns weren't tested. There was a time when *The Star* considered not continuing with the quilt books.

Edie remembers her feelings at that time: "It does not have to be this hard. We can do this. It's important."

Edie got the nod to do the next *Star* quilt book and in spring of 2000, *Star Quilts II*, was published. She's now completed seven books.

She credits the inquisitiveness of early editor Monroe Dodd with sharpening her descriptive skills. "If he didn't understand what I wrote, he made me rewrite it until he understood the concept. Now, I always write for Monroe Dodd. I don't take anything for granted."

There is not a time when she doesn't remember sewing. "There are things I don't remember not knowing how to do," she said.

Her grandmother, Laura Renner, used a treadle sewing machine. She also tatted, crocheted and made wool comforters so heavy that "as a scrawny kid, you could hardly turn over," Edie remembers.

Edie started quilting in the mid '70s because she wanted a quilt on her bed. Her first quilt was a 1930's turkey red and muslin swastika quilt. The blocks were given to her by her mother-in-law. She put them together and quilted the quilt herself.

She has always loved old quilts, especially depression-era quilts. Her friends knew of her interest and brought her feedsacks.

After collecting feedsacks for five years, she made a quilt with 175 blocks: each with a different feedsack fabric. It's backed with white feedsacks featuring logos. That quilt was finished in 1991 and was featured in Edie's *Outside the Box* book. It's also the featured project that follows.

She calls quilting both an addiction and a comfort. Divorce left Edie a single mother to raise her three sons and, "when I couldn't deal with one more squabble, I picked up my needle," she said.

She lectures about a variety of *Star* Quilts topics: how blocks illustrate historic trends such as the barnstorming years, the invention of the airplane, and patriotic quilts in the 1940s.

"I don't regret where I've ended up," she said. "I'm here in Kansas City, working at *The Star* and writing quilt books. If I had worked at *The Washington Post* or any other large newspaper, I would never have had this opportunity. I will always be grateful to *The Star* and especially to Doug Weaver, manager of Star Books, for having so much faith in me."

*Edie, age 7, in Peoria, Illinois. Her mother took this photo.*

# Pinwheels from the Past

Approximately 90" x 96"

Block size: 8"

*Hand pieced and quilted by Edie McGinnis*

*T*his is Edie's favorite quilt. She collected feed sacks for years and used 175 different ones to make this quilt. No feed sack fabric repeats. The back is made of muslin feed sacks that include company logos. The pattern, called Whirligig Hexagon, was published in The Kansas City Star in 1936. Edie finds feed sacks at estate auctions and flea markets.

## FABRIC REQUIREMENTS FOR EACH BLOCK

- One light (8" x 12")—muslin
- One dark (6" x 12")—feed sacks

## TO MAKE THE BLOCK:

- Sew A to B. Make 6 AB units for every block.

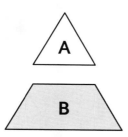

- Sew 2 sets of three units together as shown to make one half of the block.

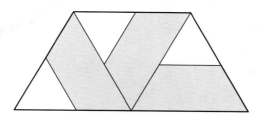

- Sew the two halves together to make one pinwheel.

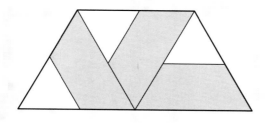

MAKE 163 WHOLE PINWHEEL BLOCKS AND 12 HALF BLOCKS.

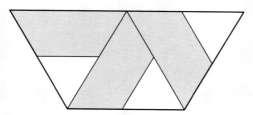

If you are machine piecing, begin sewing the halves together at the center of the block and sew to the outer edge. Come back to the center and sew to the outer edge of the block going in the opposite direction to complete the block.

If you are piecing by hand, pin the two halves together. Sew to the center and use a spider web stitch to avoid having a hole in the center of the block. The spider web stitch (see diagram) involves going through each point that meets in the center of the pinwheel. There are six points that meet. You will push the needle straight through to the next seam and again go through two points that are at an angle from each other. Push your needle through point A. Pull it up at B. Go across to C, then to D. Push your needle through to E and bring it out at F. Pull your thread tight and finish sewing across the center to complete the block. This method works no matter how many points you are trying to make meet and match at the center of a block.

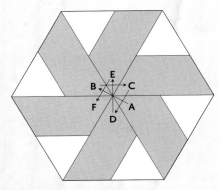

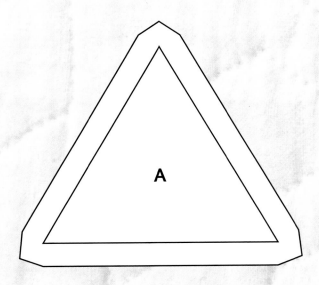

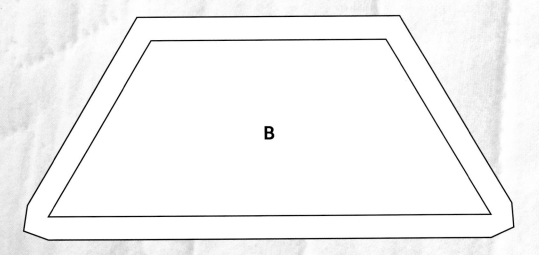

### A S S E M B L I N G   T H E   Q U I L T :

Instead of putting the quilt together in rows going across the quilt, make rows that will go lengthwise. Sew 7 rows of 13 blocks together. Join the blocks together by sewing the pinwheels together as shown.  Set these aside. Sew 6 rows together beginning and ending with a half block.

Join the rows together. Begin with a row of thirteen whole blocks. Add a row that begins with a half block. Continue on until all rows are joined together.

The edges on the sides of the quilt are pointed. The top and bottom edges are straight. When binding the quilt, use a narrow bias binding. Each point on the sides is mitered whether it is at the top or the bottom side of the quilt.

*Quilting brings Bea Oglesby's love of drawing to life.*

# Bea Oglesby

**S**he was introduced to quilting in a traditional way. She had sewn clothing for years when her college-bound daughter asked for a quilt to brighten up her drab college dorm room.

Bea learned to quilt in her no-nonsense way. An avid reader, she studied quilt books and magazines that flourished in the years after the nation's 1976 Bicentennial celebration and taught herself traditional quilt techniques.

Her love of reading and quilts came together and things have never been the same since.

In 1990, Bea designed her first quilt. It is one of her favorite quilts because it honors reading. Her three children and eight grandchildren were involved in recommending favorite books that ultimately became the 36 characters and 60 books represented on the quilt. Her daughter sent a picture of the quilt to First Lady Barbara Bush, whose dedication to literacy inspired the quilt. She responded with a handwritten note.

Ask Bea about drawing and her eyes sparkle.

"I've always drawn. I've always loved art." A high school art teacher recalling and praising her drawing skills at a reunion is a fond memory.

After the literary quilt, she turned to drawing wildflowers. Bea began making each one a quilt block. As she drew, she did research about each flower and wrote a short description about it. She called her 40 blocks a collection but others said it looked like a book waiting to be published.

She credits her engineer husband, Red, with keeping her

focused on where she wanted to go with her quilting. He would ask, "What is your goal in life?" He encouraged her to send her "collection" to a publisher.

She contacted the American Quilter's Society about publishing her work in an unconventional way. She presented them with a complete book containing 40 patterns, instructions and text for the entire quilt.

"I don't want a deadline," she said. "I might be dead by the deadline."

AQS published the wildflower book in 2000. Bea turned her energies to birds and produced 35 bird designs. They were published in 2003. Her newest book, *Butterfly Album*, was published by AQS in 2004 and includes 38 butterfly designs.

Her current interest is art nouveau designs. Memories of her childhood home in Miami-silver walls, a black grand piano, lovely vases, as well as art from the period, are her inspiration. Eighteen designs now grace her sewing room walls and she thinks that might complete her next book.

She already knows what's next. She's planning another alphabet quilt for a new grandchild. This time the quilt will feature modes of transportation.

Quilting fills her day after an early morning walk of 2-3 miles. She then writes and draws, saving her handwork for the afternoon. All of her appliqué and quilting is done by hand. "I've got the time," Bea said.

## "Do what makes you happy."

Bea likes to say, "I'm not shy" and refers to herself as an octogenarian. She's a fixture at Kansas City area quilt guilds. She has taught classes and workshops for the past ten years and lectures to area groups and quilt guilds on a variety of topics. After the literary quilt was completed, she showed it at about 50 school classes as a community service. She has volunteered regularly at the local library since moving to Overland Park when Red retired in 1989.

Before that, Red's engineering civil-service career took the family around the world: Japan, New York, California, Illinois and Missouri, Washington, DC. When she could, Bea studied weaving and oil and watercolor painting. In Tokyo, she studied the Japanese art of flower arranging, earning a certificate from the Sogetsu School of Flower Arranging.

Quilting has brought all those interests together for her. For her, it's all part of following Red's advice, "Do what makes you happy."

*Bea in Miami, 1944.*

## More about Bea...

✿ Born Jan. 21, 1924, in Pittsburgh, Pennsylvania. Parents: Lewis Sevier, writer, and Cecile Haberl, homemaker.

✿ Married Redding Oglesby, 1944, Miami, Florida. Three daughters: Corinne, Janet and Elise.

✿ College work: Home Economics, Barry University, Miami, Florida.

✿ Favorite quilt: Literacy quilt featuring 65 books with 34 illustrations.

✿ Books published:
  • *Wildflower Album,* 2000
  • *Birds & Flowers Album,* 2003
  • *Butterfly Album,* 2004

✿ Favorite quote: "Easy reading is damn hard writing" —Nathanial Hawthorne.

✿ Guild membership: The Quilter's Guild of Greater Kansas City, Blue Valley Quilt Guild, Kaw Valley Quilt Guild.

# Bee Balm

16" x 18"

*Hand appliquéd and quilted by Bea Oglesby*

**B**ee balm has many common names including Oswego tea. It was given its name by Native-Americans and was used for food or medicine long before Europeans arrived. The Oswego Indians, who came from the region of the Oswego River, drank tea from this monarda plant and taught the European settlers its uses. It was widely used after the Boston Tea Party because of the shortage of imported tea at that time. The plant, as the name implies, is attractive to bees and is also a source of delight to hummingbirds and butterflies.

There are 22 appliqué pieces in this pattern: 18 for the flower and four for the bee.

## FABRIC REQUIREMENTS

(Fat eighths measure 9" x 22", fat quarters measure 18" x 22")
- Fat eighth for background
- Fat quarter for first border
- Fat quarter for second border
- 1/3 yard for outer border
- For appliqué: green, pink, yellow and white scraps
- Black embroidery thread for bee

## FINISHED SIZES
- Background: 9" x 11"
- First border: 1/2 inch
- Second border: 1 inch
- Outer border: 2 inches

❧ Cut the center background fabric 11" x 13". This will be trimmed to size after the appliqué is finished. Center the background over the pattern and lightly trace the complete pattern onto the fabric.

❧ Draw the bee balm and the bee on the dull side of the freezer paper and cut on the drawn line. Mark each piece with its number. This is the sequence in which the pieces will be appliquéd to the background.

❧ Iron the individual pattern pieces onto the right side of the desired fabrics. Mark around each individual pattern piece with a washout marker. This is your stitching line. Cut the appliqué pieces out, leaving a 1/4" seam allowance.

❧ Remove the paper pattern, turn the seam allowance to the back and slip-stitch each piece in place on to the marked background beginning with piece #1.

❧ When the appliqué is finished, trim the background to 9 1/2" x 11 1/2". (This includes your seam allowance.)

❧ Cut the inner border one inch wide (this includes the seam allowance). Sew the border to the top, bottom and then the sides of the block.

❧ Cut the second border 1-1/2" inches wide and sew to first border.

❧ Cut the outer border 2-1/2" inches wide and sew to the second border.

❧ Mark the quilting pattern. Sandwich the top, batting and backing together and quilt by hand or machine.

❧ Stitch the details on the bee with black embroidery thread. Look at the photo to see how Bea stitched hers.

73

*Jeanne Poore was raised with quilts.*

# Jeanne Poore

She was born in her Scottish grandparent's farmhouse in Washington County, near the Nebraska border in east-central Kansas. Her great-grandfather homesteaded on land the family called the Bingo Ranch.

As a youngster, she spent most of her summers at the 120-acre farm, making good memories. She went to nearby Morrowville on Tuesday nights to watch free movies, ate penny candy, bought pop for three cents, and played with her many cousins. She slept on feather mattresses and remembers dressing by the fire on chilly mornings.

As she grew up, she watched both her grandmothers—Mildred Belle Wolf Enfield and Addah Vera Strayer Menzies—quilt. They organized quilting bees with everyone stitching on one quilt.

"I thought everybody had quilts," she said

She remembers dresses made from feedsacks. Her mother sewed most of her clothes until she went to junior high. She learned to crochet and knit and sewed clothes for her dolls.

At age 13, she finished blocks her great-grandmother gave her into a bowtie quilt. She hand pieced the blocks. It was machine quilted and given to her brother.

Her next quilt was for her son, Darryl, born in 1962. Daughter Natalie got one too. Both were embroidered quilts. She tried all the craft trends of the times. She met regularly with a group of longtime quilters in a church in Kansas City, Kansas.

In the 1970s, she started a yo-yo quilt with her sewing scraps. It went along with her for years as she drove her kids to activities; sports, scout meetings and choir practice. After putting together 3,969 yoyos, she decided it was finished in December of 1989. *Traditional Quiltworks* magazine published a picture of it in 1990.

> ## "I thought everybody had quilts."

Her desire to meet other quilters led her to join her first guild, Kansas City's Starlight Guild, in 1986. In 1987 she joined the Kansas Quilters Organization to meet more people and travel. At one of their retreats, she took a workshop with Mary Ellen Hopkins.

"She was good for me," Jeanne said. "I was raised in an era when you followed the rules. That workshop liberated me. It made it okay for me to do what I wanted to do. I realized you could use your fabric and have fun with this."

Her quilts changed after that. She began telling her students, "You don't have to please me. You have to please you."

Her lifelong knowledge of quilting techniques made her a natural to teach others. She was asked to teach techniques to fellow guild members, then taught basic quilting for Johnson County Parks and Recreation. Today she travels regularly to teach and lecture about quilts throughout the Midwest.

"I really do like the teaching. It's very satisfying seeing students succeed."

*The Kansas City Star* turned to Jeanne for quilting information for its first quilt book, *Star Quilts*, published in 1999. Since then, she has penned two of her own books. Her quilts have graced the covers of numerous magazines.

She's also been an integral part of Prairie Point Quilt Shop in Shawnee, Kansas, since it opened in 1995. She has designed the block-of-the-month series for the shop.

Work with quilt organizations—serving on the boards of both the Missouri State Quilters Guild and the Kansas Quilters Organization—rounds out her quilting activities.

That and keeping her family supplied with quilts. Special quilts are made for family members when they get married and have kids. She tries to keep a list of all the ones she has made. 1999 was a banner year, when she decided to make a quilt for every member of her immediate family—eight in all—and presented them at Thanksgiving. "Use these though the holidays," she told them. "That's what they're made for."

"I never tire of quilts. They're all interesting. I have so many favorites."

She likes traditional quilts, patterns, and antique quilts.

If you see an SUV drive by with a license plate that says QUILTS, it's Jeanne, off to teach again........

*Jeanne, age 3, with brother Gary, age 4*

## MORE ABOUT JEANNE...

❦ Born: June 25, 1942, in rural Washington County, Kansas. Parents: Keith O. Enfield, TWA instructor, and Mildred Ruth Menzies Enfield, homemaker and Hallmark employee.

❦ Married: to high school sweetheart Larry Poore, March 11, 1961.

❦ Children: Darryl and Natalie.

❦ Teacher: 6 years for Johnson County Parks and Recreation. Has taught in Arkansas, Illinois, Kansas, Missouri, Oklahoma, Nebraska, Texas and Nova Scotia, Canada.

❦ Judged quilts at: Kansas State Fair, Little Balkans Quilt Guild of Pittsburg show, Cottonwood Quilters of Nebraska show, Grand Lake of the Cherokee's guild show, Greater Kansas City Guild miniature challenge and Kansas county fairs in Wyandotte, Franklin, Anderson, Leavenworth and Miami and Johnson counties.

❦ Published: *Santa's Parade of Nursery Rhymes*, 2000; *Fan Quilt Memories*, 2001.

❦ Sources of support and encouragement: husband, children, quilt shop co-workers, fellow guild members and the Legler Barn Quilters.

❦ What she tells students: about small errors in quilts— "If you can't see it from three feet away and from the back of a galloping horse, it doesn't count. Move on, it will quilt out."

# Mildred's Nine-patch

Quilt size: 32" x 46"

Block size: 7"

*Pieced by Mildred Enfield and Jeanne Poore,*
*quilted by Jeanne Poore*

*T*hese nine-patch blocks were inherited by Jeanne from her grandmother, Mildred Belle Wolf Enfield. There are four generations of Mildreds in the Enfield family, including the person who currently owns this quilt. Jeanne Poore put it together and hand quilted it in 2001.

### FABRIC REQUIREMENTS:
* 1 yard muslin
* Varied scraps: enough to make 35 blocks

### TO MAKE THIS QUILT:
### PIECING THE BLOCKS
* Stitch the nine-patch together in rows. Stitch together the top row first using pieces C, B and C.

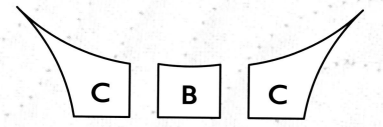

* Stitch the middle row using pieces B, A and B.

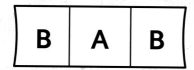

* Last, stitch together the bottom row using pieces C, B and C.

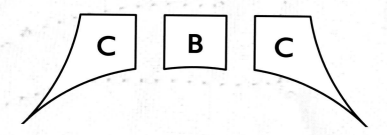

Make 35 nine patch blocks.

## CONNECTING THE BLOCKS

❧ Stitch the curved D pieces (these are the connecting pieces for Mildred's Nine-Patch) to the tops and the left side of the nine-patch only. Join all the blocks together.

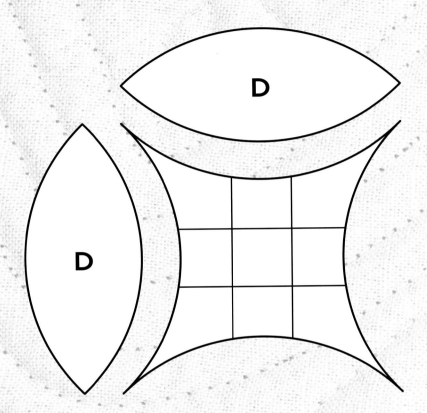

❧ Jeanne's quilt is 5 blocks wide and 7 rows deep. Add D pieces to bottom row and Ds to the right side to complete the quilt.

Jeanne hand pieced her blocks together, using muslin as the curved connecting pieces.

## BORDER

❧ The outer edges of the quilt are 6" borders. Cut them the length and width of the quilt blocks, stitch together. Appliqué the quilt edges onto the border.

❧ Cut the border edges into scallops and bind with bias-cut binding.

❧ Each block was hand quilted following its circular shape.

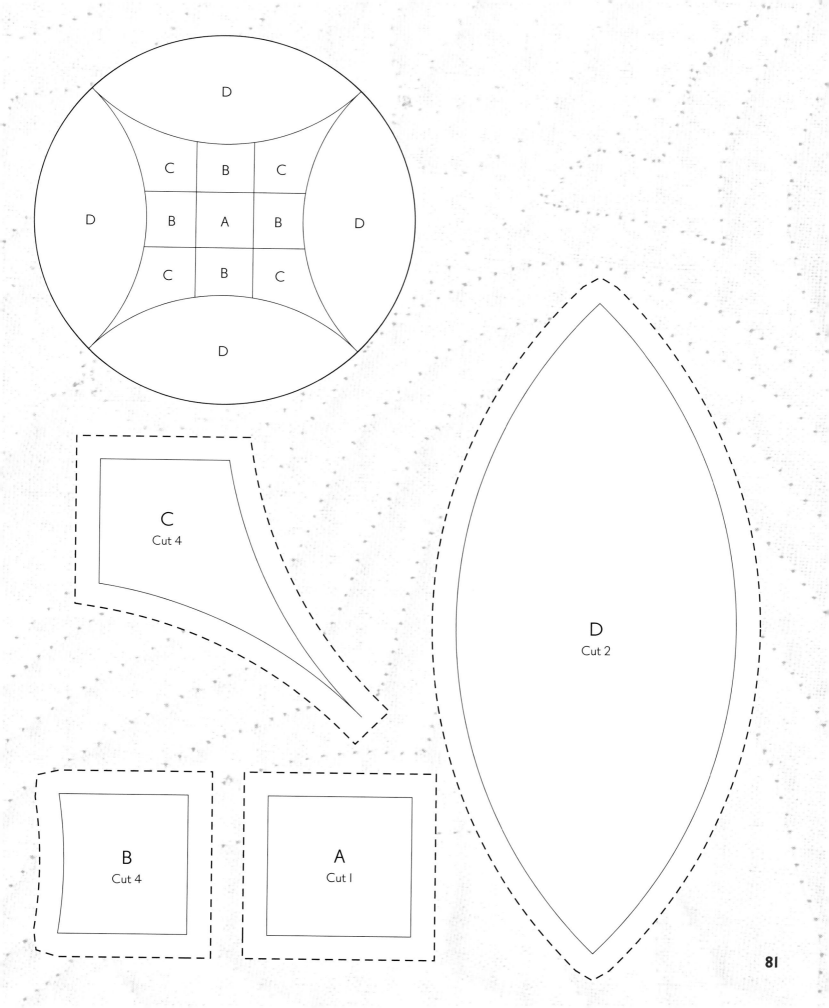

D

C B C

D B A B D

C B C

D

D

C
Cut 4

D
Cut 2

B
Cut 4

A
Cut 1

*Miriam Reed is a modest woman. She's not one who finds it easy to talk about why she has quilted most of her adult life.*

# Miriam Reed

Her quilts speak for her. They are breathtaking—expertly hand appliquéd and hand quilted in the intricate Baltimore Album style.

Miriam's dress follows the dictates of her Dunkard Brethren faith. She wears a cap on her head and simple dresses, as is the custom with those who follow this offshoot of the German Baptists and the Church of the Brethren.

Her quilts are not simple at all. She chooses rich batik fabrics for her intricate appliqué work. "I like flowers," she said. "I like the lighter colors."

When she was growing up, she watched her mother quilt. She remembers the quilting frame was set up in the living room of their home at times. Older people at their church also quilted, using quilting templates they had cut from cereal boxes.

Quilting felt awkward to her as a child. She learned the skill from her aunt, Lola Ruschhaupt and her friend Bertha Jarboe in the 1970s. They pieced quilts by hand, mostly scrap quilts for family members to use. "They used the fabrics they had," she said. Miriam's first quilt was a snowball quilt. Her second, a bowtie, was "the ugliest quilt I ever made," she laughs. Trying to escape using dull muslin, she set her blocks together with a regrettable hot pink fabric.

In 1980 she joined the Kansas City Quilt Guild, which had been formed five years earlier. She has been a member ever since. She credits the guild, taking classes and samples in local quilt shops for providing inspiration.

83

Hand appliqué appealed to her early on. "I kind of like tedious things," she said. She would relax with hand stitching in the evening.

"I'm always working at it," she said. She estimates she has made about 30 quilts.

Miriam is an anomaly in today's world: she has never had a job outside her home. "All I ever wanted to do was have a home and have a family," she said. She married when she was 17 — husband Carl was 24. "I never regretted it," she said. They have four children.

She had a cake decorating business for 30 years but she gave that up in 2000 to spend more time quilting.

> "After I put a quilt in the frame, I can't stay away from it."

Small sewing groups have also been a longtime fixture in her life.

She's been one of the "Sewing Geese" since 1980, a name fixed on the group because of their chatter. She was invited to join by Marie "Mother Goose" Hammerbacher, one of Miriam's first teachers. Eleven members met weekly for 10 years. Since then, they've met once a month in each other's homes.

"We've been through thick and thin together," she said. "You share your hurts and your joys."

She joined another group, the Baker's Dozen, in 1986. Those 13 members meet once a month in each other's homes. She remembers Mary Miller, chairman of the Kansas City Guild's quilt show, invited her to join and "it filled a void right then," she said.

She also stitches once a month with her daughter, Sandra, and two nieces who are just starting to learn to quilt.

All of them are members of the Missouri State Quilt Guild. Miriam has belonged since 1989.

Hand quilting is a special pleasure for her. "There's just something about the hand quilting," she said. "After I put a quilt in the frame, I can't stay away from it." Her frame is a traditional three-rail frame, set up occasionally in her family room.

Visitors to the Kansas City Quilt Guild's annual show in Crown Center have probably seen Miriam in action. Every year hand quilting goes on throughout the show. Miriam is the person who puts the quilt in the frame for the show. "I'm usually around the quilt frame," she said. The 2004 show was the first to feature long-arm machine quilting in place of the hand quilting, a change that Miriam realizes might be permanent.

Her most intricate quilt to date, "Through the Garden Gate," won best in show at the 2003 Kansas City Quilt Guild show. It took her three years to complete and at the urging of her friends, she will enter it into the American Quilt Society's 2005 show in Paducah, Kentucky. She and her family plan to attend the show. Another of her quilts, "Hearts and Flowers," was accepted into the juried Paducah show in 1993.

Another recent quilting challenge is the completion of quilts for all her grandchildren, "Eleven grands and eight greats!" she says. "I've got one quilt to go to be caught up, and one more great-grandchild on the way."

*Miriam, age 6, with brother Larry, age 1.*

### MORE ABOUT MIRIAM...

❊ Born August 23, 1934, in Empire, California. Parents: Harry Andrews, grocer and construction worker, and Mina Andrews, housewife, seamstress, quilter.

❊ Became interested in quilting: in 1970, from two elderly ladies from church.

❊ Married to Carl Reed, Oct. 11, 1951. Four children: Marilyn, Sandra, Duane and Donna.

❊ Influenced by: any appliqué artist, especially Elly Sienkiewicz.

❊ Honors: Quilt "Hearts and Flowers" accepted into American Quilter's Society juried show, 1993.

❊ Other accomplishments: mini-quilts stitched by Miriam were on the cover of Hallmark mini-quilt calendars in 1989 and 1990.

❊ Hobbies: gardening, sewing, cake decorating.

❊ Guild membership: Quilter's Guild of Greater Kansas City, Missouri State Guild.

# Bride's Bouquet

12" blocks

*Hand pieced and hand quilted by Mina Andrews*

*M*iriam is known for her appliqué skill, but pieced quilts handed down by family members are her sentimental favorites. One is this Bride's Bouquet, pieced by her mother, Mina Andrews, in the 1940s. Patterns calling this block the Bride's Bouquet and the Nose Gay Quilt were published by the Rural New Yorker in 1933. It was published as "The Nose Gays" in The Kansas City Star in 1937.

Mina's quilt contains 32 complete blocks and 16 partial blocks. Hers is mostly scraps, but the yellow and blue pieces throughout unify this quilt. She finished it with two plain borders, one muslin and one blue.

The Bride's Bouquet quilt pictured measures 70" x 83". Its blocks measure 11" square. Our templates will make the more common size block of 12", in case you want to mix and match blocks. Hence, your finished quilt will be larger than Mina's.

Directions follow for piecing one block:

### FABRIC REQUIREMENTS:

- Fat eighth for background
- Fat eighth yellow
- Fat eighth blue
- Varied scraps for bouquet pieces

### CUT

A—2 yellow (reverse 1), 2 blue (reverse 1)
B—6 light/medium prints
C—5 light/medium prints
D—4 light background
E—6 light background (reverse 3)

### STITCH

Piece together the pieces that meet in the center:
- Stitch 2 B diamonds together. Make three sets.

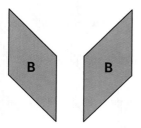

- Stitch 1 yellow A to 1 yellow Ar as shown.

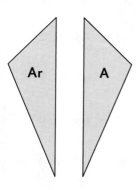

Next piece 3 E-C-Er units. These units will fill in three of the corners of the block.

❧ Stitch a C piece to an E then add an Er. Make three of these units.

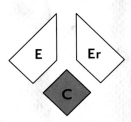

❧ Stitch I D triangle to a C square. Add another D triangle as shown. Make 2 of these units.

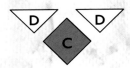

❧ Join all units together like this:

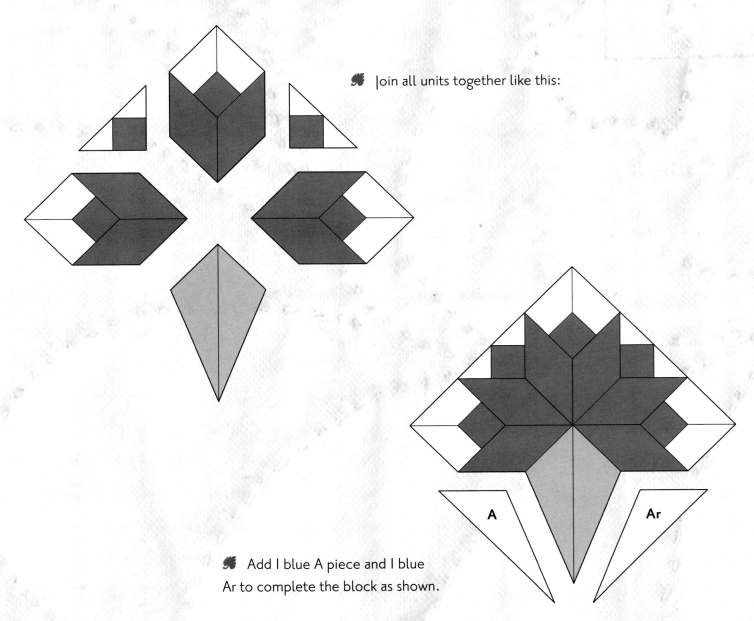

❧ Add I blue A piece and I blue Ar to complete the block as shown.

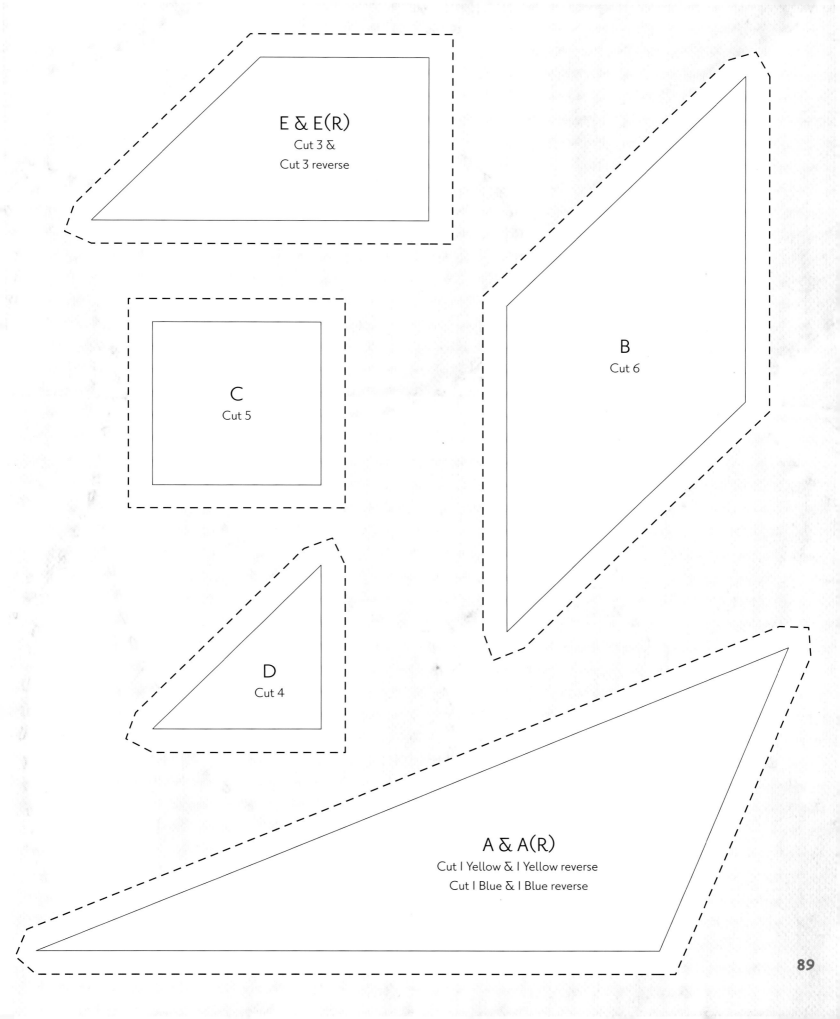

E & E(R)
Cut 3 &
Cut 3 reverse

B
Cut 6

C
Cut 5

D
Cut 4

A & A(R)
Cut 1 Yellow & 1 Yellow reverse
Cut 1 Blue & 1 Blue reverse

Terry Clothier Thompson had never made a quilt in her life when she agreed to teach a quilting class in 1972.

# Terry Thompson

Quilts have been a part of her life ever since. She's been a quilt shop owner, an antique quilt dealer, a chronicler of quilt history, a quilt appraiser, a pattern designer and a quilt book author—so far.

That first class, a continuing education class at Johnson County Community College, attracted 35 eager students. *One Hundred and One Patchwork Patterns* by Ruby Short McKim was their textbook.

Their interest in quilting spurred Terry and friend Cindy Taylor Clark to open one of the first quilts shops in the Midwest in 1973. The Quilting Bee was located at 45th and State Line in Kansas City. They started with a Christmas consignment sale, and offered handmade quilt related gifts. From there, they moved to 45th and Bell. Terry remembers getting a $500 loan to begin the business, chipping in $50 for muslin, and ordering 10 bolts of cloth from the Eli Walker Company.

By that time, "I'd really started studying," about quilts, Terry said. She pored over *Quilts in America* by Myron and Patsy Orlofsky to learn about quilt patterns and dates. Old quilts were plentiful then. Intricate quilts could be purchased for $75.

Many will remember the quilt shop Terry operated on the Country Club Plaza from 1977 to 1984. The Quilting Bee merged with another Plaza quilt shop, Quilt Country, in 1979. Besides retail sales, they designed patterns and operated a wholesale business upstairs from their Seville Square shop.

In 1984, Terry sold her share of the business and moved to Colorado. She dabbled at selling antiques in Leadville. She drifted away from quilts, but a move to Denver and work at a quilt shop there brought back a flood of memories about why she enjoyed the quilt business.

"It reminded me that quilts help women find themselves and their creative side," she said. "You see their faces light up because they've made something with their hands. It's so beautiful and you're part of a community of women."

Several events converged to bring Terry back to Kansas.

She inherited the Peace Creek family farmland near Hutchinson. She also met Nancy Hornback, who recruited her to work on the Kansas Quilt Project in 1986.

"The project brought me back from the dead," she said. She felt like she was part of the quilt world again, as she helped document approximately 1,700 quilts in central and western Kansas. Soon she was reprinting her quilt patterns, designing her own shopping sacks to market her business and teaching beginning appliqué at several nearby community colleges.

"Teaching is my favorite," she said. "I tell my students not to take out their beginning stitches, to just continue to sew. With practice, their appliqué and piecework will begin to be consistent and even."

Terry is a wellspring of ideas. "They never stop," she says. "I love giving lectures. It's a performance in a way. I let the quilts tell me what to say." Working with historian Barbara Brackman on the Kansas Quilt Project changed her teaching style. Now she combines history with quilt instruction. "My teaching combines my interest in women's history and quilts. Students sew and discuss the daily activities of women's lives in different periods of history," she said.

> "Quilts help women find themselves and their creative side."

Becoming a grandmother, combined with a divorce, prompted her to leave the farm and move to Lawrence in 1991.

Terry now teaches locally and writes books for her own pattern company and for Kansas City Star Books. She also designs reproduction fabric for Moda Fabrics with Barbara Brackman. Her home studio in Lawrence, where she teaches weekend workshops, houses a vast library of historical books and vintage fabrics.

*Terry at age 7*

❧ Born February 8, 1944, in Stafford, Kansas. Parents: Willard Clothier and Esther Richardson, homemaker, Mark Richardson (stepfather), geologist.

❧ First memory: being carried by her grandfather Wilford Clothier to look at family pictures on the walls.

❧ Married at age 18 (for 19 years), two children, Shawn and Shannon. Married at 43 (for five years).

❧ Early influences: grandmothers Reka Clothier and Vera Clothier, mother Esther Richardson, aunt Betty Kinnamon.

❧ Childhood aspirations: to be a cowgirl and raise horses and cattle on a ranch in Arizona with cousin Carol Jo Kinnamon; OR to be a singer and movie actress.

❧ Influenced by: early quilt books, especially Jean Ray Laury's *Appliqué Stitchery*.

❧ Greatest satisfaction: to inspire women to quilt for their own reasons: for personal satisfaction, to escape from family duties, to enjoy handwork

# Wild Rose Mourning Quilt

36" x 36"

*Stitched by Jean Stanclift, quilted by Pam Mayfield*

*T*erry's ancestors homesteaded and farmed near Hutchinson, Kansas. They called their community Peace Creek. Terry designed this small quilt to honor unnamed infants buried in her family's prairie cemetery there. She found roses carved on many of the little headstones and included them in her design. Use your favorite method to appliqué the rose wreath in the center block.

## FABRIC NEEDED

- 2/3 yard for one 20" background square
- Fat quarter red for roses and buds
- 1/2 yard green for bud calyx, wreath and stems
- Scrap of yellow for center of roses
- 8-10 fat quarters of black, brown and tan for border blocks

## CUT

- 1 - 20 1/2" square using background fabric
- 136" of one-inch bias strips for wreath and stems
- 4 roses
- 4 rose centers
- 3 buds
- 3 calyx
- 56 - 4 1/2" squares for border

## Appliqué block

🍀 Using a 1/2" bias tape maker, make 1/4" finished bias strips.

🍀 Following photo for placement, lay two strips for the wreath in a simple meandering circle. Pin in place.

🍀 Add 8 strips (8"-10" long) for stems of roses. Arrange them to cross each other, as in the photo. Pin in place.

🍀 Sew the centers of the roses in place.

🍀 Place roses in each corner, covering the ends of the stems. Pin in place.

🍀 Sew 3 calyxes to buds. Pin in place inside wreath.

🍀 Baste and appliqué all to background.

Note: Terry's original quilt had strips pieced to the edge of her background block. Cutting a 20 1/2" x 20 1/2" block will make this unnecessary.

## Border

🍀 Sew the squares into strips. Make four strips of 5 squares. Sew two strips together for the top and two strips for the bottom. Next, make four strips of 9 squares each. Sew two strips together and attach to each side.

## Finish

🍀 Quilt and bind.

🍀 If yours is also a mourning quilt, inscribe the name of the person being remembered.

🍀 Sign and date your quilt.

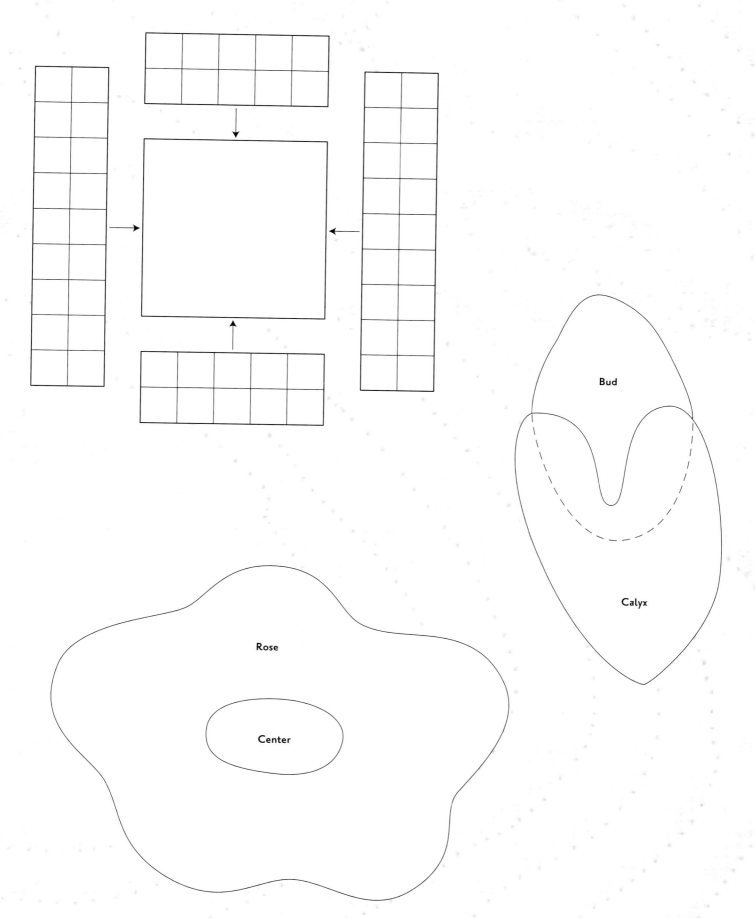

Bud

Calyx

Rose

Center

*Nancy Wakefield's eyes twinkle when she says, "My parents were scary. I come from a very organized family. You followed the rules, period."*

# Nancy Wakefield

**S**he inherited those organizational skills and applies them to many aspects of her life, one of them being the Heartland Quilt Network, a fast-growing Midwest quilt networking organization. She's been president of that group for the past two years.

"I'm a person that understands organizations," she said.

This is also a woman who genially admits, "I'm the general," for running family life throughout her husband's 30-year military career.

Nancy will admit quite frankly, "I quilt for mental health. Not only was I raising a child with special needs, but my husband's career required him to be away for long periods of time."

Nancy's first love is piecing quilts, but she is branching out and doing some appliqué work. "I like scrap quilts and I love the old quilts," she said. She has great admiration for our quilting foremothers. "Those women had no training, no tools, no newly purchased cloth like we have—and look what they accomplished," she said.

One of those women was her paternal grandmother, Allie Mae Page. Born in Ohio in 1865, nearly 6-feet tall, Allie moved to Kansas and was the town dressmaker in Gorton, Kansas, until she met James Page when she was 35 years old. They married at high noon on January 1, 1900, moved to Wagner in Oklahoma territory and bought a farm. James was a bookkeeper and built roads; she ran the farm. They had three children before she was 40—Allie

> ### "Those women had no training, no tools, no newly purchased cloth like we have—and look what they accomplished."

employed a nanny to care for them while she worked. Times were hard and they worked hard.

Nancy clearly loves Allie's life story. "I admired her so much. Look at her life! She was a career woman in a dual income family and had child care. Who says any of this is new?"

In Allie's golden years, James took over the farm duties and she quilted. She was part of a group that met every Wednesday. Their quilts were made from *Kansas City Star* patterns. Nancy has many of Allie's quilts today.

Nancy made her first quilt for her daughter in 1967 and remembers working on more quilts in 1975. While they were stationed at Fort Riley, Kansas, Nancy was instrumental in setting up the Konza Prairie Quilt Guild in Manhattan in 1978. In her free time, she earned a master's degree in counseling from Kansas State University. She began teaching quilting classes and making quilted items for sale during those years in the Flint Hills.

Working and military moves kept her from quilting from 1984 to 1991. She kept up with quilt trends but missed out on the rotary cutter, new fabrics and new books.

In 1993, she went to work at a Virginia quilt shop, the Quilt Patch. When Nancy told them she was partially color blind, they had her work the desk. Her skill in helping customers who brought in old quilts soon became evident. She can't see blended colors like aqua, purples and browns but she can see color values.

After Tom retired, they relocated to Platte City, Missouri, near Leavenworth, Kansas, in 1997. It was their 17th move. Nancy made a pillow inscribed, "It's hard being the colonel's only troop."

Nancy quickly became involved in a number of quilt groups: the Northland Quilters Guild, the Quilter's Guild of Greater Kansas City and the Kaw Valley Quilter's Guild.

She enjoys testing quilt patterns for a number of designers, including Judy Robb and Nancy Graves, Elly Sienkiewicz, Barbara Brackman and Terry Thompson. Quilts she wants to make next include one using only William Morris fabrics, chintz quilts and more scrap quilts, especially string quilts.

She is currently president of the Heartland Quilt Network, an organization that connects quilt guilds, quilt shops, and quilt professionals across the Midwest—Arkansas, Iowa, Kansas, Missouri, Nebraska and Oklahoma.

Heartland is not the only organization Nancy is involved with. "I do this for my church too," she said. She's also served as president of her local homes association.

"I keep saying no. They keep saying please.........." She believes that if you belong to an organization and benefit from it, you need to give back to that group by working on committees or in a leadership role.

*Young Nancy in Oklahoma.*

## MORE ABOUT NANCY...

❀ Born December 27, 1940, in Lawton, Oklahoma. Parents: George and Jane Page, phone company manager/educator.

❀ Married to Tom Wakefield, January 25, 1964. Two children: Stacy and Elizabeth.

❀ Influenced by: paternal grandmother, Allie Page.

❀ Education: B.S. in math education, Oklahoma State University. M.S. in counseling, Kansas State University.

❀ Special interests: Nancy and Tom adopt retired greyhounds and spoil them rotten for the golden years of their lives.

❀ Accomplishments: one of the founders of the Konza Prairie Quilt Guild in Manhattan, Kansas; president, Heartland Quilt Network, 2002-present. Has served in guild leadership positions: program chair for three guilds, treasurer for two guilds, bazaar chair and quilt show co-chair.

# Truly Nancy

76" x 78"

*Hand pieced by Nancy Wakefield*

Nancy's love of piecing and reproduction fabrics made her proclaim this quilt to be "truly Nancy" so we decided that would be its name. She pieced it by hand, using die cut paper pieces for patterns (see source list, page 137). It took two years to complete, as it was her handwork project carried to quilting bees and guild meetings.

It's a one-patch quilt, meaning you only need one pattern piece — a 1 1/2" hexagon. Nancy basted her fabric to the paper patterns, then stitched pieces together using a buttonhole stitch on the back to keep them lying flat. That also kept her paper patterns from bending and she could re-use them once she removed the basting stitches.

Nancy's quilt has 859 pieces. She began with a dark center, then added hexagons of

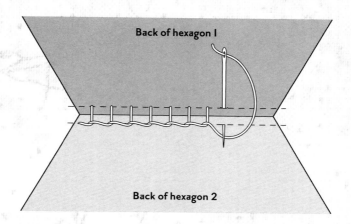

Back of hexagon 1

Back of hexagon 2

light, dark and medium color values.

An 8" reproduction fabric border completes her quilt.

To make your own hexagon quilt, begin with a dark center. Sew light hexagons around the center. Next, add dark hexagons, then medium. Continue in this manner until your quilt reaches the size you want. You will then need to add hexagons to each corner, following the same color arrangement as above (light, dark, and medium). When Nancy finished her quilt, she trimmed the outside edges. You need to go back and secure those hexagons with stay-stitching before adding the border.

(Note the picture of Nancy on page 99. She is holding another hexagon quilt she hand pieced. Those pieces are one-half inch hexagons.)

1¹/₂" Hexagon

*"It's time to start rounding up things for the big trip."*

# Maebelle Walkenhorst

**M**aebelle Walkenhorst may be slowed by a recent stroke at age 82, but her memory is sparkling clear.

She can describe piano lessons at age 8 with Pearl "Miss Pearl" Glover. She recalls that her room and board during high school in the '30s was paid with potatoes. She hasn't forgotten that her high school graduation dress was velvet, which she liked, but black, which was a disappointment.

She remembers sitting by the treadle machine while her mother sewed. She cut out pieces for her mother and prepared them for pressing with a heavy "sad" iron. Her mother's quilts were mostly heavy comforters made from old wool clothing. They were used on the beds in the upstairs of their house where there was no heat. All were tied with carpet warp thread.

At the two-room country grade school she attended in Henley, Missouri, students worked on hobbies every Friday afternoon. The teacher taught her to quilt in the 6th grade. With fabric her mother provided, Maebelle remembers making a bowtie quilt.

She took some quilting classes in the '50s, "kind of playing around with quilts" by her own admission. She remembers buying three used dresses and making a quilt from them. "I always felt proud because my sister did that—made beautiful things out of everyday items. She could make a silk purse out of a sow's ear."

Maebelle started teaching in 1941. She taught kindergarten for 29 years, then college level classes for Central Missouri State University for seven years.

"I love to teach," she said. "I love to see the light of recognition when they learn something."

Maebelle's family pitched in to remodel her garage so she could continue teaching adult education quilting classes for Longview College while caring for her husband as he battled Parkinson's disease. She furnished the machines for those classes, Singer featherweights she had collected over the years.

"Quilt making was my sanity during my husband's long struggle with Parkinson's disease," she said.

She has recently completed a project she inherited at the 1998 annual meeting of the Missouri State Quilter's Guild—that turned into a six-year saga. Maebelle organized a project to distribute "comfort" quilts to worthy organizations.

Since then, 744 quilts have passed into the hands of local charities: the Missouri State Highway Patrol, Truman Medical Hospital's pregnancy unit, the Women's Clinic of Kansas City and the Linus Connection.

She was surprised when the Missouri State Quilter's Guild recognized her efforts in April 2004. Maebelle was named the first inductee into their Galaxy of Stars. She often helped with registration at their meetings and organized their first quilt show in the Missouri State Capitol rotunda in 1995.

Her sewing room in her Lee's Summit home is neat as a pin. Fabric is arranged by color, and boxes of unfinished projects await her attention. "There I can relax my whole self," she said. Every Thursday night is quilt night at Grandma's, with two daughters and one granddaughter with a special interest in quilting in attendance. Everyone brings their own projects to work on.

> "I just have fun with life. If you don't have fun, it's your own fault."

She has collected and made many quilts over the years and is concerned about where her legacy will end up. "It's the quilts that have them all in a stew", she said. She has left instructions in her will that any not chosen by her family go to the Missouri Baptist Children's Home.

Her favorite quilt is one made of feed sacks with 452 pieces.

She commemorated the millennium with a "2000" charm quilt with 2000 pieces.

"I've done enough sweatshirts to robe the town."

"Now here I am nearing the end and quilting is my first love," she said.

*Maebelle in 1945.*

## MORE ABOUT MAEBELLE...

❀ November 4, 1922, in rural Cole County, Missouri. Parents: Frank Hoskins, farmer and Cora Hoskins, mother, housewife, women's community club and 4H leader.

❀ Became interested in sewing: helping her mother, who passed away when Maebelle was 15. Her older sister Bernetta got her hooked on quilting.

❀ Married to: "my Bill" Walkenhorst, August 10, 1945, "when he returned from Europe." Four children: Cheryl Ann, Kris, Freda, Edwin.

❀ Influenced by: "I learned most from my failures."

❀ Education: attended grade school in a two-room school in Spring Valley. Degrees from Southwest Baptist College, University of Missouri at Kansas City and Central Missouri State College (masters in education specialist).

❀ Other accomplishments: first inductee into the Galaxy of Stars, Missouri State Quilters' Guild, spring 2004.

❀ Taught quilting: for local guilds and shops, adult education classes.

❀ Guild membership: Missouri State Quilter's Guild since its inception in 1988, Lee's Summit Guild, Quilter's Guild of Greater Kansas City, Pleasant Hill Night Guild.

# Maebelle's Heart Blossom

*Stitched by Jean Stanclift, quilted by Pam Mayfield*

32" x 32"

*M*aebelle Walkenhorst designed this floral appliqué block and created this pattern in 1993.

## FABRICS NEEDED (6 TOTAL)

- 1/2 yard background fabric
- 1/4 yard of 2 coordinated fabrics for flowers, buds and hearts (our sample uses fat eighths of 8 coordinated fabrics)
- 1/4 yard green for stems/leaves
- 1/4 yard for inner border
- 1/2 yard for outer border
- Binding

## CUT

- 14 1/2" square background
- 4 strips 1 5/8" x 18" for inner borders

(The extra length is for mitering the four corners. If strips are cut straight of grain it will give greater strength for joining the bias edge of the corner triangles. Strips may be cut cross-grain but great care must be taken not to stretch as the bias edge is attached.)

- 2 - 12 1/2" squares background fabric

Mark a diagonal line from corner to corner on each square. These will make the four corner triangles. The diagonal line will be the edge joining the narrow floral border around the center square. It works well to appliqué the corner motifs before the squares are cut in half on the diagonal line, thus preventing stretching the bias edge while the appliqué is being completed.

- 4 - 2 3/4" x 30" outside border strips (will finish 2 1/4" x 28")

(The extra length is for mitering corners.)

- 4 - 9" strips of 3/8" wide bias
- Appliqué pieces

## CENTER SQUARE

❧ Fold the 14 1/2" square diagonally and lightly crease. Fold a second diagonal line and mark the center of the square.

❧ Trace pattern pieces on freezer paper, marking on the dull side of the paper. Cut out. Place the shiny side on the wrong side of the fabric. Press in place and cut out the pieces, adding 1/4" seam allowance.

❧ Turn under and glue the seam allowances to the freezer paper. It's not necessary to turn them under in places that will be under other pieces. (These places are indicated with dotted lines on the patterns).

❧ Stitch the hearts and circle onto the center blossom.

❧ Arrange the pieces as shown in the photo. Center the large blossom on the background fabric. Place pieces 1, 2, 3 and 4 on the diagonal fold lines and pin or baste them in place. Appliqué. (Pieces 1, 2, 3 and 4 should be appliquéd in that order.)

❧ Add the narrow border around the center square. Miter corners.

## FOUR CORNER TRIANGLES

❧ Place the bias stems in place according to the placement diagram and photo.

❧ Arrange buds, bud tips and leaves.

❧ Pin or baste all in place.

❧ Appliqué.

❧ Cut the diagonal line of the two squares to make the four triangle corners. Pin and baste the long side of the triangles to the floral strips, matching the centers. Stitch.

❧ After all the appliqué is complete, trim away the background fabrics behind the appliquéd pieces, leaving a 1/4" seam allowance. Remove the freezer paper. Where there are layers of appliqué, trim the fabrics as you come to them.

❧ Add the outside borders, matching the centers. Stitch the borders only to the seam line at each corner. Miter the corners.

## TO FINISH

❧ Mark the wallhanging with a quilting design of your choice. Baste the lining, batting and top layers together. Quilt. Add binding and a sleeve for hanging.

Enjoy!

—Maebelle Walkenhorst

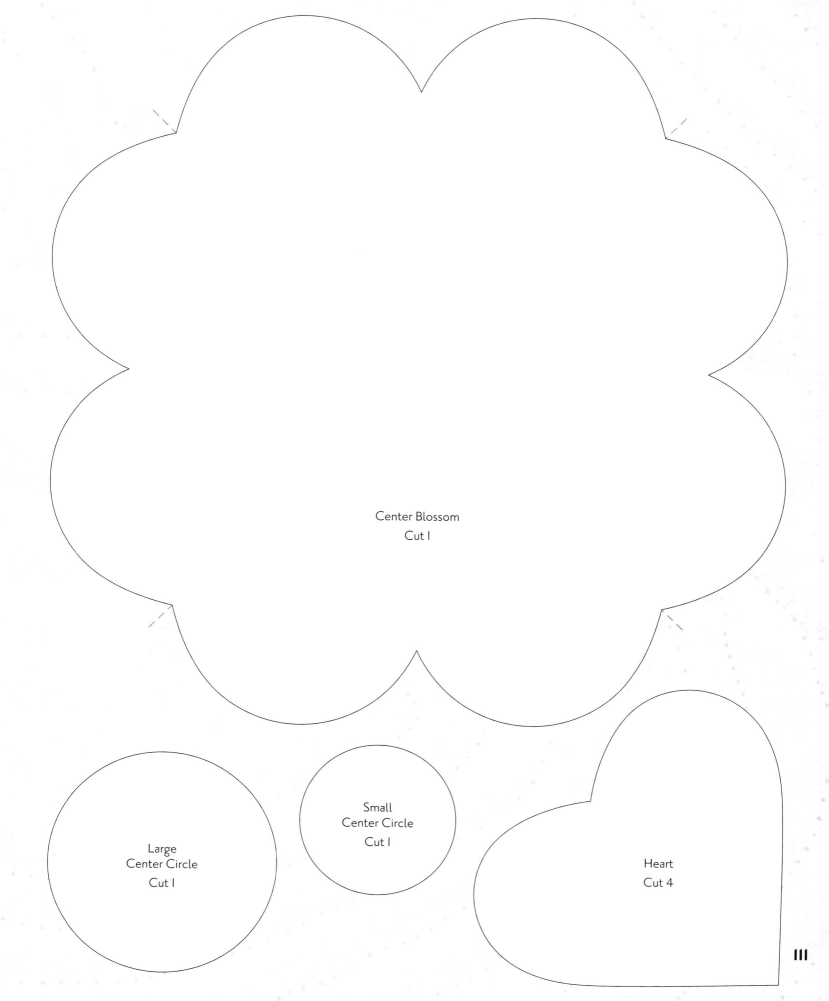

Center Blossom
Cut 1

Large
Center Circle
Cut 1

Small
Center Circle
Cut 1

Heart
Cut 4

III

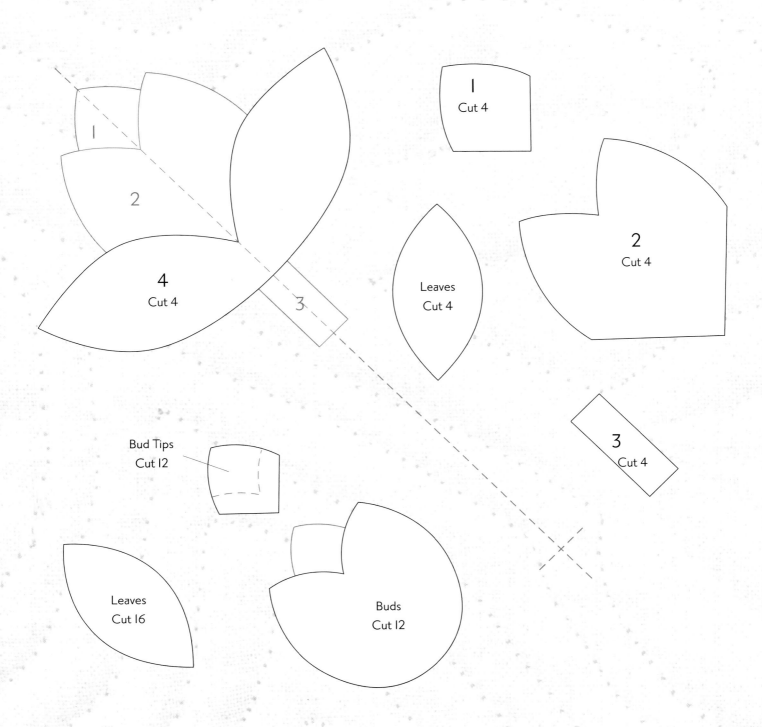

1
Cut 4

2
Cut 4

Leaves
Cut 4

2
Cut 4

3
Cut 4

1

2

4
Cut 4

3

Bud Tips
Cut 12

Leaves
Cut 16

Buds
Cut 12

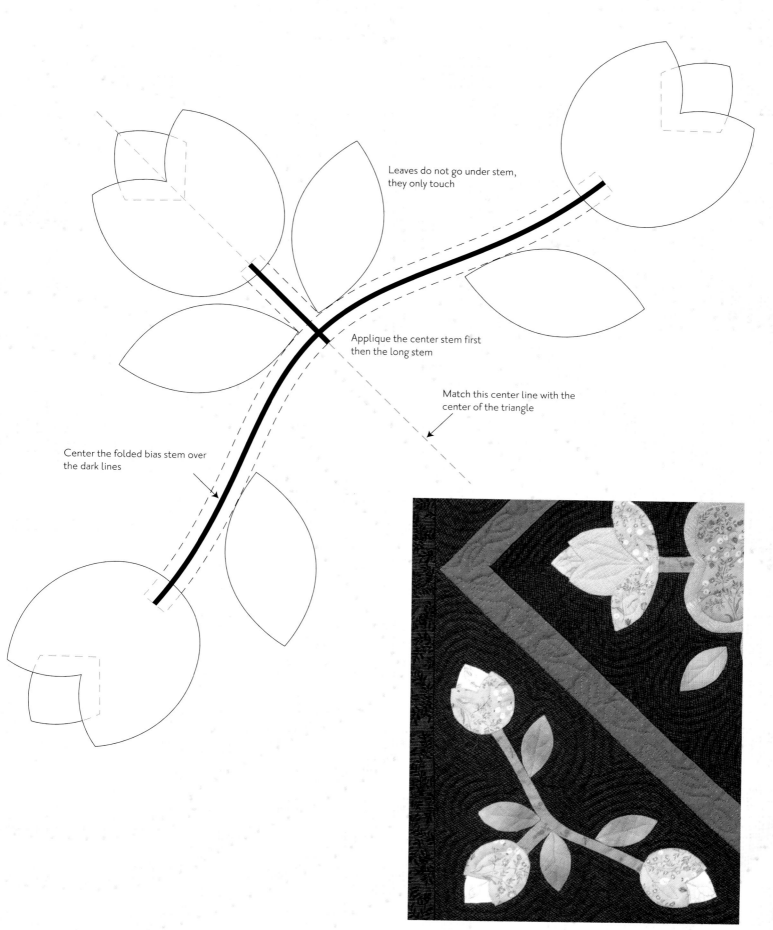

Leaves do not go under stem, they only touch

Applique the center stem first then the long stem

Match this center line with the center of the triangle

Center the folded bias stem over the dark lines

*Everyone should be lucky enough to know someone like Iris Werner.*

# Iris Werner

**H**ers was a house often overflowing with humanity, as she raised seven kids and welcomed their many friends running in and out of her house.

What we didn't realize was that all the while, she never stopped making art.

She kept a log of the art she gave away "because I knew I wouldn't remember," she said. The small book lists the quilts she has given away: 36 baby quilts, five friendship quilts, 85 comforters and 90 quilts. It also lists the paintings she has given away, along with 18 cat tote bags, 50 cat t-shirts.....

In the front of the book, she wrote, "On the occasion of my finding a three-yard-for-a-dollar fabric sale—I need the reinforcement of thinking of all the quilts and comforters, etc. that have sprung from my rooms—boxes—sacks of miscellaneous scrap."

Her scraps now reside in a room in her home that few are allowed to enter. We suspect the door won't open completely.

It's a long-kept collection. She remembers her grandmother, Mary "Mame" Roseman, trying to teach her to quilt. Grandma Mame used feed bags, and embellished her comforters with big purple butterflies. Iris remembers listening patiently to her, even though her childhood interest in quilting was mild.

When her kids were young, she started piecing quilts with scraps left over from clothing she sewed for them: shirts for the boys, matching Easter dresses for the girls. "It was nice to remember their clothes," she said.

And when people found out she made quilts, they would give her their fabric scraps.

"I tried to say no, but when I opened my lips, I said yes," she said. "Now, I have enough stuff to make quilts for the Army."

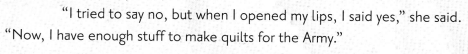

> ## "Whenever I cut into something that might have some more use, I tell myself 'I am immortalizing it.'"

Shiny fabrics, gingham, and neckties all go into quilts that are gifts to celebrate weddings, graduations and other celebrations. "People say they don't remember who gave them most gifts, but about quilts, they say 'I remember who gave me that,'" she said.

Stacks of quilts wait in one closet of her home to be given away. Her love of cats inspired a hunt for and collection of fabrics featuring cats. Cat quilts were made for each of her 15 grandchildren — there is a stack of them waiting for their wedding day. The quilts are made in simple patterns. Each block uses some cat fabric and most of these quilts feature a large cat. "It reinforces that I'm the cat grandma," she said.

Most of her quilts are unplanned: "catch as catch can," Iris calls them. She often works at her machine with piles of scraps around her to add as she pleases.

She considers quilts with dark colors to be more handsome. Her favorites are a series of comforters with all darks, but with a piece of red in every block. Every quilt has one fabric that shines or has something embellished on the surface.

There are other planned quilts she remembers: one that was like a flag, another log cabin quilt that was all light tan and unbleached fabrics, mostly plain, but every block had one strip of shiny blue fabric. "I still have that fabric and I would probably do another one of those one of these days," she said.

Earlier retirement days were spent sewing and listening to Dr. Laura on the radio. But now, "my sewing machine doesn't work as slick as it used to," she said.

These days Iris paints more than she sews. "It's easier to get to the paint," she explains. Her sun-filled dining room is her studio. She is surrounded by buckets of brushes, stacks of paper, a window filled with blue glass bottles and vases. She paints every day. Irises are a favorite subject, as are cartoons and cards.

I seldom leave her house without something she has made to take along and savor......

*(Note: The author was one of those lucky friends of Iris's daughter Lisa. The house where we gathered while growing up is the historic Bluejacket Lodge at 9904 Hocker Drive, Merriam.)*

*Iris Logan, age 21, nursing student at St. Luke's Hospital, Kansas City, Missouri.*

By Iris Logan Werner

The fun of a quilt is deep in my heart.

I see my grandmother pointing out different fabrics.

"This was a sun suit I made for you."

"I made three little shirts for the boys out of this gingham."

"Your mama had some bloomers from this feedbag."

The traditional thing is that one uses the scraps—leftovers—from sewing our children's clothing. Sometimes an article of clothing was outgrown or disfigured—leaving a lot of "good" fabric and twice as many memories. Whenever I cut into something that might have some more use, I tell myself "I am immortalizing it."

At first, I would only use my own leftover pieces, but when friends were breaking up housekeeping, moving or just trying to run a tight ship, they would give me a call.

"Iris, do you want my material?" I have to struggle, but I usually end up saying yes leaving me with a delightful assortment of someone else's memories. The back room where these treasures have been placed is not to be viewed by anyone who is still in a state of fertility. I always tell them, "I'm afraid it will make your eggs go bad." Carefully, I keep the curtains drawn when the lights are on or I might have been asked to leave the neighborhood long ago.

When I sit down to piece a crazy quilt, it requires me to sit in a sea of oddly shaped pieces, saying, "Choose me. Choose me!"

I have a given a lot of my friends quilts and comforters, many as wedding gifts or baby quilts. Some one told me after being married for 10 years, "I have forgotten who gave us all of our wedding presents, except for the comforter you gave us."

My life has been fulfilled in nearly every way possible. I always knew I wanted to be a nurse, a mother and an artist. I had seven children. Not one of them is spoiled or greedy. I worked as an RN in the emergency room and other departments. Job? No, more than that, a love. I have 15 grandchildren and since I have a big tender heart for cats, they call me their "cat grandma." I have made each of them a quilt—heavily featuring cats—for their wedding presents in case I am not around. I had them hand-quilted by Margaret Bartlett, a lady in Arkansas who was featured in the television show, "A Simple Life." She is 80 and lives alone on a farm.

I think nothing feels as delicious on a bed as a quilt. I even love the Chinese imported quilts but 1/8" seam allowances don't make them last long. Along my journey, I have embraced the Catholic faith, have so many friends and in spite of an era of ill health, I am glad to be here and grateful to God for my multiple blessings.

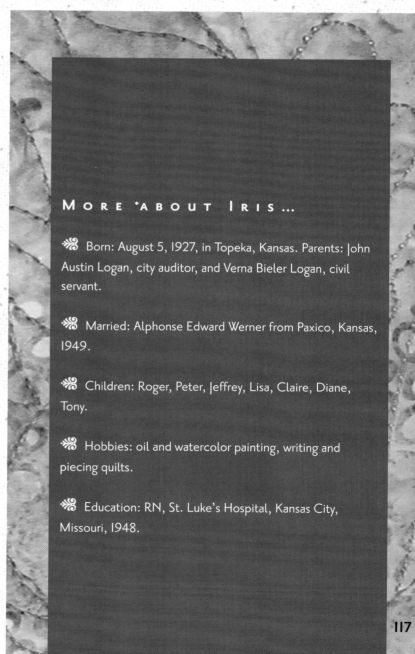

## MORE ABOUT IRIS...

❀ Born: August 5, 1927, in Topeka, Kansas. Parents: John Austin Logan, city auditor, and Verna Bieler Logan, civil servant.

❀ Married: Alphonse Edward Werner from Paxico, Kansas, 1949.

❀ Children: Roger, Peter, Jeffrey, Lisa, Claire, Diane, Tony.

❀ Hobbies: oil and watercolor painting, writing and piecing quilts.

❀ Education: RN, St. Luke's Hospital, Kansas City, Missouri, 1948.

# A Quilt of False Starts

72" x 84"

*Pieced by Verna Logan and Iris Werner, quilted by Faye Dodd*

ris's favorite quilt is sentimental. "I took a potpourri of quilt blocks made by my mother, Verna Bieler Logan. I put them in the center of a square, turned them on point and filled the rest of the square with strips and scraps that combined old sentiment and new," she said.

She pieced it after Verna died in 1978. She calls it a quilt of false starts: blocks her mother pieced but never finished. Each block of the quilt begins with one of her mother's blocks and is surrounded by strips of Iris's scraps. All were stitched to a paper foundation, which acts as a stabilizer. It was removed after the block was stitched.

Each block measures 13" and is bordered by a tiny 1/2" wide border print. This quilt is a great way to preserve sentimental blocks you may inherit.

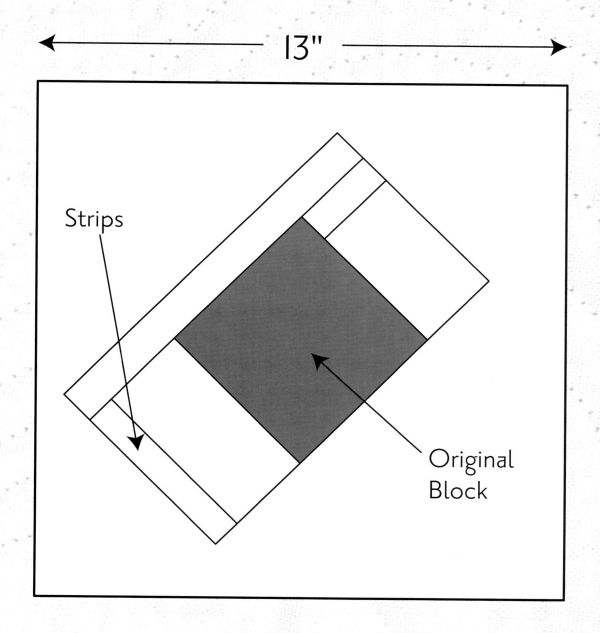

← 13" →

Strips

Original Block

# Bizarre Batik

*Pieced by Lou Gehlbach, machine quilted by Rosie Mayhew*

Quilt size: 38" x 54" • Block size: 10"

*L*ou Gehlbach created this batik version of A Quilt of False Starts. She chose a
rich batik for the background fabric. Blocks from Iris's original strip-pieced
quilt were the inspiration for her batik blocks. She turned to her collection of batik fabrics
and used colors she found in the background fabric. This quilt lets you use up batiks in your
collection and gives you a chance to play with color.

Here's how Lou made her quilt:

## FABRIC REQUIREMENTS

- ❧ Blocks: use scraps of your choice. The more you have, the better.
- ❧ Background/binding: 1 3/4 yards

## BLOCKS

Lou began each block with a center block inspired by one she saw in Iris's quilt. She
set that block on point and stitched strips randomly around it, pressing and trimming
as she added each one. She continued adding strips until the block measured
10 1/2" x 10 1/2". She made six of those blocks.

## BACKGROUND

- ❧ Cut: 9- 6 1/2" x 10" strips. Stitch these between and to sides of blocks.
- ❧ Cut: 4 - 6 1/2" x 38" strips. Attach these to tops and bottoms of rows.

## TO FINISH

These borders provide a space for fancy quilting to shine. We told Rosie Mayhew
"the sky's the limit" for whatever quilting designs she felt inspired to try. She added
intricate "feathered feathers" and fun flowers atop each pieced block.

*"That's all I do now,"* Lavon Wynn says.
*"Every free minute I get, I make quilt tops."*

# Lavon Wynn

Now that she has retired, Lavon is spending her golden years in the same way she spent her childhood—quilting.

When she was growing up, Lavon's mother, Mary Broyles Brown, and her grandmother, Stella Ellison, both quilted in the little country town of Savannah, the county seat of Hardin County, in Tennessee.

Lavon's mother told her she started sewing when she was 3 or 4 years old. Lavon remembers working alongside the adults, making doll clothes. When she got older, she cut out patterns for them from paper bags. Another job was tearing the paper backing off string quilts for her grandmother. That wasn't her favorite task. She can remember quilts they made: The Fan, Grandmother's Flower Garden, Colonial Basket, Double Wedding Ring, Nine-Patch, Irish Chain and Ocean Waves.

"Mother made a pattern over and over if she had success at it," Lavon said.

All their quilts were hand pieced and hand quilted. They used commercial patterns and whatever fabric they had on hand.

"We weren't going to throw anything away," Lavon said. "Whatever little scraps we had, we used. Many of the scraps came from dress making. Sometimes, not often, we did buy fabrics especially for quilt making."

She still has one of her grandmother's quilts and quite a few made by her mother.

Lavon's career as a home economics teacher put her quilt making on hold—except during the summer months. "Most of the

123

time, I completed a quilt every summer. Sometimes I worked on a quilt top for two or three summers before I could get it finished," she said.

She taught clothing at Sumner High School early in her teaching career. Her daughter's birth and her husband's military career interrupted her teaching until 1974. She then resumed teaching at Washington High School in Kansas City, Kansas, where she taught clothing, the family as a consumer, interior decoration and foods. She retired in 1995.

## "There's always one more quilt you've just got to have."

She was inspired to make two versions of the 2004 *Kansas City Star* block of the month quilt. "It seemed like a good idea at the time, but now I am not so sure," she said.

Scrap quilts are her favorite.

"It's like taking something that would ordinarily be thrown away and making something useful out of it. It's a challenge to make the useful item pretty too. You have to learn how to balance your lights and darks, your dulls and brights, your large-scale prints and small-scale prints, your plaids and stripes. They (my mother and my grandmother) put everything in a quilt," she said.

Lavon likes to make quilts in pieced, traditional patterns best. Books and magazines give her ideas. When she likes a block, she makes a test block to see if she wants to make an entire quilt of that pattern. Last year, she donated 30 blocks to her guild auction that she didn't want to make into quilts.

"I can't finish all the quilts that I want to make in my lifetime," she reasoned.

She has about 30 completed quilt tops. Her plan is to stop piecing and concentrate on machine quilting some of those tops. She successfully quilted a small wall hanging on her regular sewing machine and now wants to try a larger quilt.

"I'm looking forward to switching over from the quilt top making to the quilting because I think I've got enough quilt tops. I never thought I'd say that!" she said.

Lavon meets regularly with several small quilt groups in her Kansas City, Kansas, neighborhood.

"It's about my entertainment now," she said.

A group calling themselves the Scrappy Bunch is one. "We work a little and talk a little," on every third Wednesday of the month, she says. "Then we go to lunch." The group was originally organized by a Wal-Mart fabric department associate. They have met together for more than three years.

Another group of quilters meets every Monday. "They pulled me out of retirement for advice and haven't stopped asking," Lavon said. The quilt making members of the First Baptist church of Quindaro, where her husband, Lemuel, is pastor, meet at the Quindaro Community Center.

Lavon doesn't see any end in sight to her interest in quilt making. "There's always one more quilt you've just got to have."

*Lavon with her mother, Christmas 1943.*

Quilt size: 60" x 75" • Block size: 12" x 12"

*Hand pieced and hand quilted by Stella Ellison, 1899-1994*

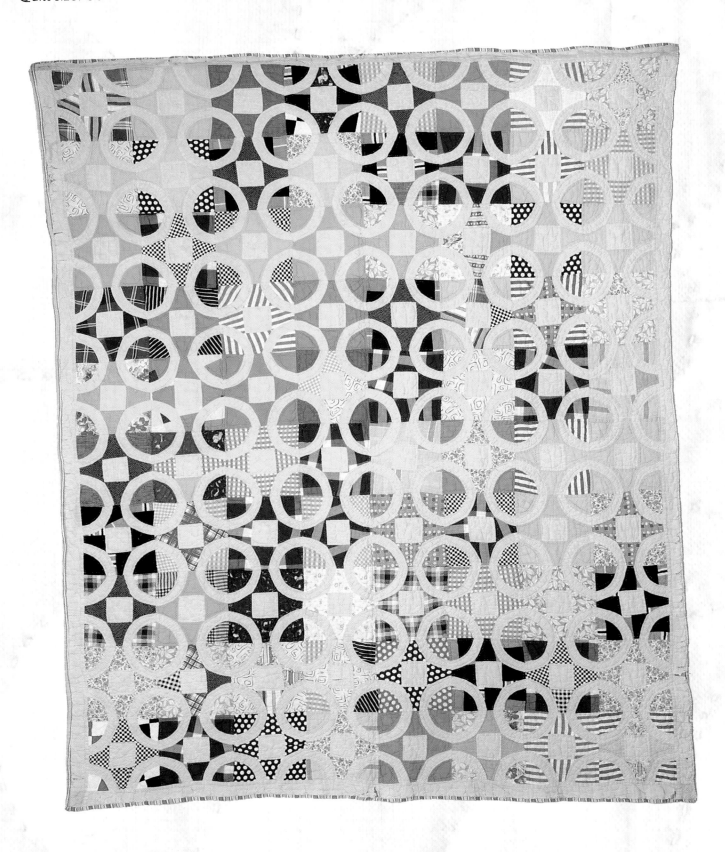

*L*avon's daughter says yellow is a happy color so we are calling this the Happy Quilt. Lavon's grandmother, Stella Ellison, pieced it in the 1940s in Tennessee. The pattern, called A Friendship Quilt, was published in The Kansas City Star on May 2, 1945. It has also been called the Block and Ring Quilt by Aunt Martha's patterns.

We give you instructions for piecing one block. Stella's quilt has 80 7" blocks. Her use of different fabrics throughout makes this a very happy quilt. If you examine the photo closely, you will see that she used the same fabric for the centers and rings throughout. When she had enough fabric, she used the same fabric for the rest of the block pieces. Sometimes, she uses one fabric for the pieces that join the center and another fabric for the corner pieces. Stella was unafraid to work off the straight of the grain and also used some very large prints, which adds to the excitement and movement of her quilt.

Our block measures 12" for easier and faster piecing. (Note: we do not recommend working off the straight of the grain.)

## FABRIC REQUIREMENTS:

- Fat eighth yellow
- Varied scraps

## TO PIECE THE BLOCK:

### CUT

- 4 A pieces
- 4 B pieces
- 4 C pieces
- 1 D piece

### STITCH

Stitch the C pieces to the center D square.

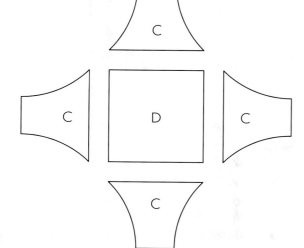

Next sew the B pieces to the A pieces, making 4 AB units.

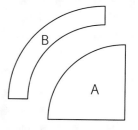

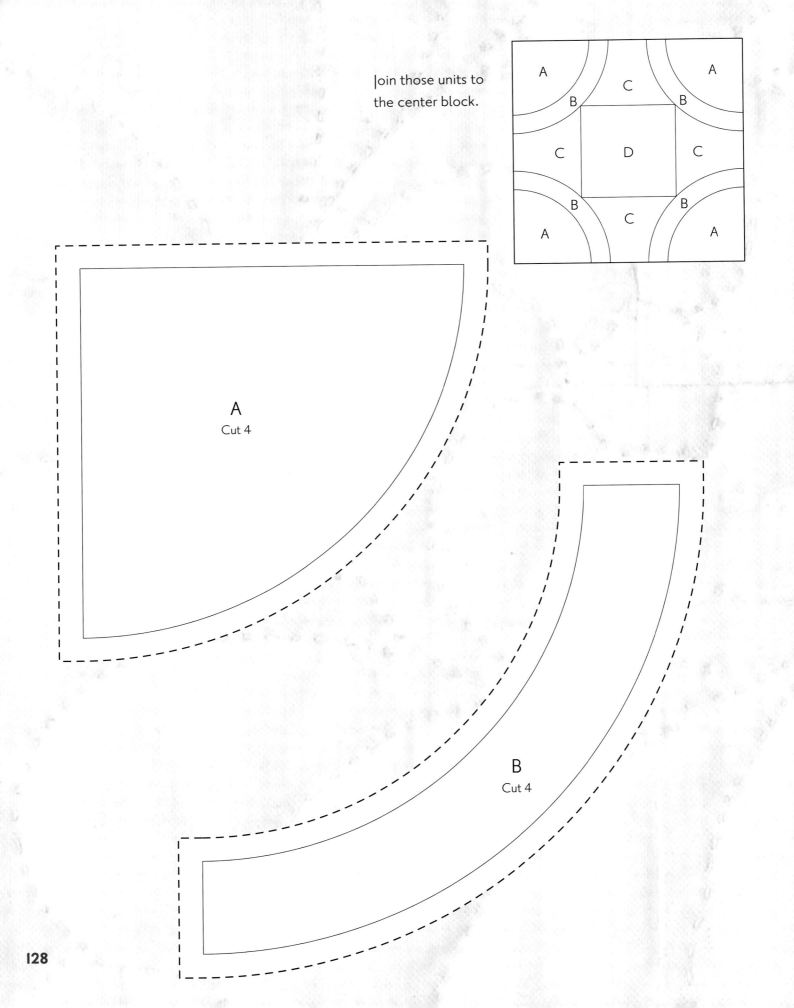

Join those units to the center block.

A
Cut 4

B
Cut 4

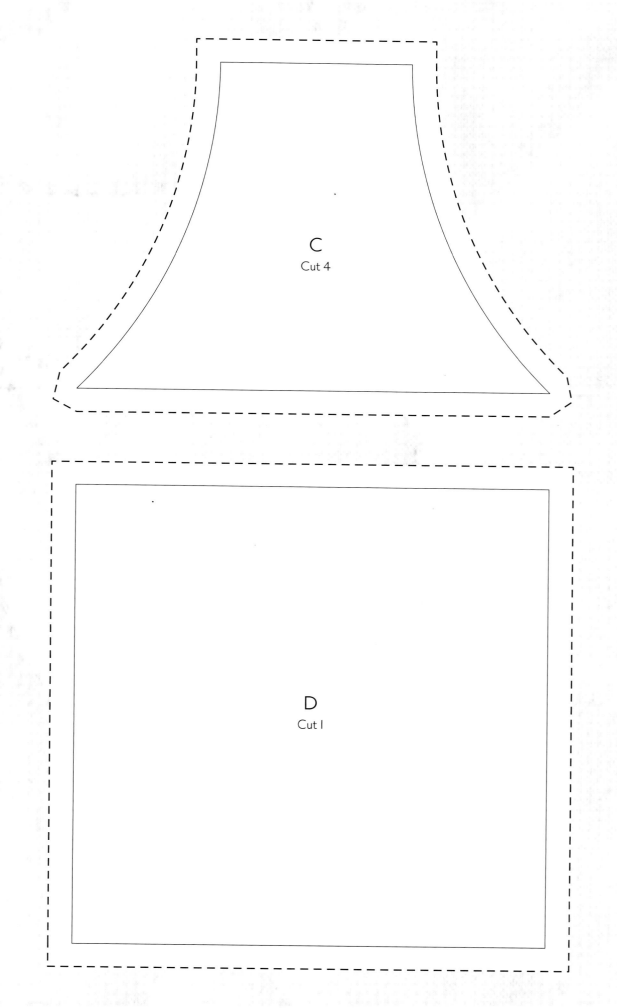

C

Cut 4

D

Cut 1

*Women, it is often said, have rarely told their own stories. Our experience… has shown us that women recorded their own stories through their needlework, their writing, and the tales they told their children. It is only now, at the end of the twentieth century, that we are ready to listen.*

—Kansas Quilts and Quilters, University Press of Kansas, 1993

# How to collect stories

The aim of this book is to encourage people to collect stories about quilters. The quilters in our midst are leaving a legacy that will be passed down for generations to come. Some day, a lucky recipient will wonder about the quilt's maker. Who was she (or he)? What did she like? What happened to her in her lifetime?

There are many ways to collect stories. You don't necessarily have to be a writer to do it.

### COLLECT ARTICLES AND INFORMATION ABOUT THAT QUILTER

Start a file folder for your favorite quilter and when something is written about them, save a copy of it. It's a simple way to compile information for future reference.

### ASK QUESTIONS

"I wish I knew more about those people." Jeanne Poore was curious about who signed the friendship quilt she inherited from her mother. In her search to learn more, she talked to her dad and older brother. She found names and connections for three-quarters of those people who signed her mom's quilt.

## TAKE NOTES

When you visit, jot notes of dates, names and comments made. Notes are valuable reminders of what was said. If you type them up soon after your interview, you will make them more complete and polished for future reference. You will also find questions you didn't ask that you can follow up on later.

## RECORD VISITS ON TAPE

Collecting an oral history is also valuable. Record your conversations and save the tape, noting the participants, the date and the place of the visit. See the references section for more sources of information about collecting oral history.

## YOU MIGHT MAKE A NEW FRIEND

Asking others about themselves can have an unexpected benefit: you could gain a new friend. Besides collecting information, this is a way to strengthen a relationship you already have—or build a new friendship.

Some quilters visited with prolific quilter Lucyle Jewett, around the time of the 1978 Kansas Quilt Symposium. Lucyle observed:

"Each occasion was a red letter day, so far as I am concerned. It was a mutual 'show and tell' affair and we could talk freely without fearing to bore anyone; no quilt person is bored talking about, or hearing others talk about quilts."

—from *The Quilting Records of Rachel Adella Jewett and Lucyle Jewett*, by Sara Reimer Farley and Nancy Hornback, *Uncoverings* 1997, Research Papers of the American Quilt Study Group

# Interview guide

*Research is formalized curiosity. It is poking and prying with a purpose.*

—Zora Neale Hurston

**This interview guide was given to each of the quilters in this book. They were encouraged to fill out as much as they wanted. It is intended to be a guide to spark memories.**

Your name
Address
Phone
Email
Personal Information
Date, place of birth
Parents' names
Father's occupation, achievements
Mother's occupation, achievements
Siblings (name, birth date)

## CHILDHOOD
Where, housework, chores, meals, playtime, preferred activities
What is your earliest memory?
What were times like when you were a child?
What types of things did you do as a child?
School: liked/disliked, key teachers, friends, favorite subjects
Grade school
High school
College
Early goals, hopes—what did you want to be when you grew up?

## ADULT LIFE
First job(s)
Marital history
Date of marriage

What did you do for a living?
Where did you live?
Children's names
Activities
Travel
Interests

## QUILTING
When did you start?
How did you learn?
Influential classes
Teachers
Early projects
Books that influenced you
Who influenced you?
Early work
How/when did it change?
Visions/epiphanies
How does quilting make you feel?
Why do you quilt?
Greatest satisfaction
Greatest disappointment
Favorite type of quilting: piecing? appliqué?
Favorite quilt

## GOALS
Published work
Achievements
Guild membership
Sources of support, encouragement

## WHAT DID I FORGET TO ASK?

# What my Dad remembers

When he was growing up in the 1930's, my dad, Walter Roy Gehlbach, remembers his grandmother, Mary Schrader, doing more quilting than his mother. "Mom was probably too busy taking care of the kids to quilt much," he said.

Mary Schrader lived in a central Illinois community of mostly German farmers. Homes were generally within 3/4 mile of each other, Dad said. They lived on what were called family farms, smaller farms of 80 to 160 acres, which produced enough for a family to survive on. Theirs was six miles northwest of Lincoln, near New Holland.

Dad remembers the quilting frame going up every winter in his grandma's living room. There was a potbellied stove on one side of the room. The frame was set up in front of that stove. The frame consisted of sawhorses holding 1" x 4" boards with c-clamps on the corners. The 1" x 4"s would be pulled tight to stretch the quilt out. There were chairs set around all four sides of the quilt. The frame was up all winter long.

When it was cold outside, women would gather to quilt during the day. Kerosene lamps were their only light in the evenings. Besides stitching, the gatherings allowed the neighbors to "keep up with what was going on in the area," he said. Walt remembers playing under the quilt frame, sitting on the couch reading and watching the women work. His brother, Bill, thinks they probably played there because that room was about all they heated in those days.

*(Author's note: While I was working on this book, I asked my mom what she remembered about her relatives quilting and my dad surprised us with this story. I had never heard it before.)*

## DOCUMENTING YOUR QUILTS

Our quilts are intertwined with our lives. They document our interests, our hopes, our joys. They comfort us when we know we just have to keep on going, to put one foot ahead of another to get through tough times.

Some quilts are precise and exquisitely planned. Others are clearly a project picked up in snatches of time, completed in precious moments of free time in a busy woman's day. Some quilts are for show. Others are unmistakably for use.

You can't help but wonder about the maker. Was she a sweet woman? Was she a spunky one? Were her quilting hours happy ones? Was she retreating from a world of hurt and heartache?

Here are some tips for documenting your quilts:

## WAYS TO DOCUMENT YOUR QUILT

### LABEL IT

Information to include on a label:

※ Date: When the quilt was/is presented or the period during which it was made.

※ Pattern name: list the name of the pattern or note that your design is original.

※ Name of quilt maker

※ City and state

※ Recipient's name

※ Occasion commemorated by this quilt (wedding, birthday, graduation, etc.)

※ What was your inspiration for making this quilt?

### MORE LABEL SUGGESTIONS

※ A label can identify your quilt if it is lost or stolen. Adding the label before the quilt is quilted will make it even more permanent. Working your initials into the appliqué or piecing are good permanent labels.

※ Labels can also include care instructions for cleaning, which can guide a recipient who is unfamiliar with the careful care and cleaning needed for quilts.

※ Check the permanence: If you use a pen, test a scrap to make sure it won't wash out.

### WRITE ABOUT IT

※ Keep a quilt journal. Many quilters keep records of the quilts they have made, complete with photos and notes.

# References

*Envelopes of Sound: Six Practitioners Discuss the Method, Theory and Practice of Oral History and Oral Testimony*, edited by Ronald J. Grele, 1975, Precedent Publishing, Inc., Chicago, Illinois.

*Kansas Quilts and Quilters*, Barbara Brackman, Jennie A. Chinn, Gayle R. Davis, Terry Thompson, Sara Reimer Farley, Nancy Hornback, 1993, University Press of Kansas, Lawrence, Kansas.

*Like It Was: A Complete Guide to Writing Oral History*, by Cynthia Stokes Brown, 1988, Teachers & Writers Collaborative, New York, N.Y.

*Oral History: An Introduction for Students*, James Hoopes, 1979, The University of North Carolina Press, Chapel Hill.

*Record and Remember, Tracing Your Roots Through Oral History*, Ellen Robin Epstein and Rona Mendelsohn, 1978, Sovereign Books, New York.

*Women's Work: The First 20,000 Years. Women, Cloth and Society in Early Times*, Elizabeth Wayland Barber, 1994. W. W. Norton & Company, Inc. NY, NY.

## WEB SITES

You can find out more about quilters in our area and collecting stories through these web sites:

http://www.jocolibrary.org/index.asp?DisplayPageID=23
Johnson County, Kansas' Library system provides this page of information about quilting.

http://www.quiltguilds.com/kansas.htm
List of quilt guilds throughout the state of Kansas

http://www.quiltguilds.com/missouri.htm
List of quilt guilds throughout the state of Missouri

http://heartlandquiltnetwork.com/
The Heartland Quilt Network connects quilt guilds, quilt shops and professionals across the Midwest. It shares information about programs, workshops, shows and events to promote the popular and enduring art of quilt making.

http://www.kshs.org/portraits/johnson_osa.htm
A delightful listing of people through time who have a connection with Kansas history.

www.livingtreasuresproject.org
This project is making a record the Northwest's most important and influential elder craft professionals—of their lives, their work and their achievements.

# Source list

### PAPER PIECES

Nancy Wakefield recommends using templates available from Paper Pieces for accurate English paper-piecing like that in her project, "Truly Nancy." Paper Pieces has a web site: www.paperpieces.com. Their address is P.O. Box 68, Sycamore, IL 60178. Phone: 800-337-1537 or 815-899-0925.

### FABRIC PAINTING

Paint: Chris Wolf Edmonds recommends Createx paint. You can reach them at 1-800-243-2712 to request a color chart and price list. You can order by phone and they will ship promptly. For more information, check out their web site: http://www.createxcolors.com/. Their address is Createx Colors, 14 Airport Park Road, East Granby, CT. USA 06026.

Fabric: Call Testfabrics at 570-603-0432 for swatch books and prices. They also have a variety of silks available which can be painted and printed with the same products as cotton. Their web site is http://www.testfabrics.com/index.html.

### A SPECIAL THANKS

The antique quilting items pictured throughout this book were graciously loaned by Sue Breeding of Mayhew Antiques in Marysville, Kansas. To contact the shop, call 785-562-5110.

# "Why do I quilt?"

I quilt for sentimental reasons. It's a way of keeping good memories around. The first quilt I made was for my dorm room bed at college. It was made from the sewing scraps from my two best high school buddies and myself.

I made a quilt for my best boyfriend, the one I married. I love a picture of him holding it, grinning from ear to ear in the San Francisco airport.

I made quilts for my daughters—flannel quilts, t-shirt quilts, throws we worked on together. I made a pocket quilt for my favorite nephew.

I made quilts for my brothers, of flannel shirts we'd all worn over the years. They are threads you hope will hold your family together over time.

There are quilts I've made to welcome babies. My favorite ones include scraps of the new parent's shirts. There are quilts for children we don't know, ones who are sick or who need some comfort as they begin preschool.

Quilting has also helped me through darker moments. Nancy Hornback told me, "It holds me together." That's true for me, too. News of my brother contracting AIDS came in the gloom of a German wintertime in the dark, early days of the epidemic. On the heels of that news, my young daughters got chicken pox, one after the other, keeping us isolated and alone for weeks. Work on a quilt got me through those dark days. I named it "After Chicken Pox Comes Spring."

Another quilt commemorated my brother's death. It was made as a panel for the AIDS quilt but it never got farther than my mom's bedroom. It's still there today.

My grandma made me quilts. My mom made me quilts. I carefully save them all.

Sign your quilts. Date your quilts. Leave a record of what held you together.

*Debra Gehlbach Rowden is a quilt author and editor. She has a degree in mass communications/clothing and textiles and enjoys combining her passion for words and fabric at every opportunity. This is her second Kansas City Star book. She lives in Lawrence, Kansas.*

# Other Star books

Star Quilts I: *One Piece at a Time*
Star Quilts II: *More Kansas City Star Quilts*
Star Quilts III: *Outside the Box: Hexagon Patterns from The Kansas City Star*
Star Quilts IV: *Prairie Flower: A Year on the Plains*
Star Quilts V: *The Sister Blocks*
Star Quilts VI: *Kansas City Quiltmakers*
Star Quilts VII: *O'Glory: Americana Quilt Blocks from The Kansas City Star*
Star Quilts VIII: *Hearts & Flowers: Hand Appliqué from Start to Finish*
Star Quilts IX: *Roads & Curves Ahead*
Star Quilts X: *Celebration of American Life: Appliqué Patterns Honoring a Nation and Its People*
Star Quilts XI: *Women of Grace & Charm: A Quilting Tribute to the Women Who Served in World War II*
Star Quilts XII: *A Heartland Album: More Techniques in Hand Appliqué*
Star Quilts XIII: *Quilting a Poem: Designs Inspired by America's Poets*
Star Quilts XIV: *Carolyn's Paper-Pieced Garden: Patterns for Miniature and Full-Sized Quilts*
Star Quilts XV: *Murders On Elderberry Road: A Queen Bee Quilt Mystery*
Star Quilts XVI: *Friendships in Bloom: Round Robin Quilts*
Star Quilts XVII : *Baskets of Treasures: Designs Inspired by Life Along the River*
Star Quilts XVIII: *Heart & Home: Unique American Women and the Houses that Inspire*
Star Quilts XIX: *Women of Design*
Star Quilts XX: *The Basics : An Easy Guide to Beginning Quiltmaking*
Star Quilts XXI : *Four Block Quilts: Echoes of History, Pieced Boldly & Appliquéd Freely*
Star Quilts XXII: *No Boundaries: Bringing Your Fabric Over the Edge*
Star Quilts XXIII: *Horn of Plenty for a New Century*
Star Quilts XXIV: *Quilting a Garden*
Star Quilts XXV: *A Murder of Taste: A Queen Bee Quilt Mystery*
Star Quilts XXVI: *Stars All Around Us: Quilts and Projects Inspired by a Beloved Symbol*

## PROJECT BOOKS:

*Santa's Parade of Nursery Rhymes*
*Fan Quilt Memories: A Selection of Fan Quilts from The Kansas City Star*